SIXTY MINUTES
TO A LIFETIME

Sixty Minutes To A Lifetime

Lessons I've Learned About Life and Football
from My NFL Coaching Career

Bob Slowik

CSP

A Conscious Shift Publication
Conscious Shift Publishing Registered Offices: Saint Petersburg, FL 33710

Library of Congress Control Number: 2017943571
Robert S. Slowik
Sixty Minutes To a Lifetime
Lessons I've Learned About Life and Football from My NFL Coaching Career/
Robert S. Slowik
ISBN 9780997955248
ISBN 0997955244

Published in the United States of America
Book cover design by Ellen Kaltenbacher
Book cover images courtesy of licensing agreement with Bigstock by Shutterstock
Interior graphics by Lauritzen Slowik

DEDICATION

I dedicate this book to my children Ryan, Andrea, Bobby, and Steve; and my grandchildren Tye, Averie, Natalie, and future grandchildren. I hope some nuggets of wisdom I learned on my journey will turn into gold for them as they did for me, in navigating life's winding road.

I also want to dedicate this book to all those passionate, dedicated, and hardworking assistant coaches you will never hear about, but who commit their careers to positively influencing those they coach.

TABLE OF CONTENTS

PREFACE

M Y FIRST EXPERIENCE playing organized football was so real. The anticipation, anxiety, excitement, and the contact were elements that came together to create an experience I couldn't resist. My size limited my potential on the football field, but football had me hooked. The level of intensity, training, and competitiveness was beyond any I had experienced before stepping on the field.

Football was demanding, difficult, grueling; and only a few had the mental, physical, and emotional make-up to stick with it. Doing something difficult was rewarding and made me feel as though I was part of a special group. Being a member of a team and working towards one common goal was also something that motivated me. Football is man vs. man, it is a world of collisions, a world with obstacles, and intrigue -- a team game like no other.

Those years of sixty minutes on the field inspired me to continue the game as a coach. Sixty minutes has turned to a lifetime of playing, coaching, and now writing about my experience.

Football is a lot like life and life is a lot like football. I hope to bring you into the world of coaches and competitors at the pinnacle of their profession. To provide inspiration and lessons for competitors of all kinds looking to gain an edge with a variety of game day mindsets -- whatever your game.

I would like to present messages of hope, determination, and passion for anyone in the game of life. The most important lessons I've learned: Success is not <u>what</u> you do for a living, success is <u>how</u> you live what you do! Have a Passion for Good and do Good with a Passion.

With that mindset, you will find yourself not only striving to be good, but looking for good in whatever environment or circumstances you create. You will then most likely find it. I have found that changing my perspective has helped me feel truly alive, so I CAN LIVE what I do!

A Coach's Life: The Early Years of My Coaching Journey

After nearly thirteen years in college football I was blessed with one of the most exciting opportunities in my coaching career. I was fortunate to become a member of the Dallas Cowboys coaching staff in 1992. Dave Wannstedt was a high school classmate who climbed the coaching ranks to become Jimmy Johnson's defensive coordinator. His recommendation got me an interview and I landed a job as a defensive assistant -- an entry level coaching role that blossomed into becoming the nickel coach. That first year was one of the most grueling, yet rewarding of my coaching career.

We won Super Bowl XXVII with a score of 52-17 over Buffalo to become World Champions. That catapulted me into my twenty-year NFL coaching career.

The story that led up to that championship and the following years was not that simple.

Prior to my job with the Dallas Cowboys, I spent thirteen years in the college ranks. I started as a graduate assistant at my alma mater, the University of Delaware. From there I became a volunteer assistant at the University of Florida where my wife was the women's head track coach. A year later I was hired for what was called a part-time position: part-time is a little misleading. It meant working beyond the hours of a full-time coach with a lot less pay. We had only one car which my wife used for work. I would jump on a bus at 5am and catch the last available returning at 11:45pm. Her season was year-round. I was trying to break into the ranks as a full-time coach and that kept me at the office trying to impress. We spent four years at the University of Florida and rarely saw each other except to sleep and wake up to go to work. The NCAA eliminated the part-time position and forced us to a new adventure at Drake University in Iowa. My wife Carol was about to give birth when I went off to Drake and recruiting. Once recruiting ended I made it back to Gainesville to load a small U-Haul truck. Carol drove the Honda hatchback with our kids, two-year-old Ryan and our infant daughter, Andrea. That made for a lot of stops and bottle feeding. I drove that U-Haul with the muffler dragging on the road the whole way, until I had to tie it up with my belt because it was throwing sparks and lighting up the night road. I was actually concerned it might catch the truck on fire. We made it and moved into a two-bedroom apartment.

That year was a real learning experience. We won only one game and rumors of dropping football were flying. I had a chance to interview for another job at East Carolina University, but would have to resign my position at Drake to do so because I had promised to be there for two years. After talking with my wife Carol and doing lots of soul searching and prayer I resigned and then interviewed. I didn't get the job. So, there we were in Des Moines, Iowa with two young babies, no job, and nothing but a small income from Carol's part-time coaching position. We had some savings to live on for a few months. My time was spent from December to March calling school after school, coach after coach, and receiving rejection after rejection trying to find a job. We were close to running through all the savings and decided we had no choice but to move to Carol's parents' home until we found employment.

Time to rent another U-Haul and load the few belongings we had. I did have to recruit some help to load the truck, but I had yet another financial and logistical dilemma. We needed a driver for the U-Haul, a driver for our Honda, and a driver for a beat-up Oldsmobile Toronado that got me to and from my recruiting areas. Another issue besides a third driver was gas money for the long drive from Iowa to Delaware. We were desperate enough that I asked one of my young moving helpers if he was interested in buying a car. I let him test drive the car which ran well; I always kept the Toronado very clean. "How much?" was the next question. "One hundred dollars and the title," I said. Sold! If he didn't buy it I was going to leave it in the parking lot with the keys and a handwritten sign on the dashboard "Finders Keepers".

As we were about to load the truck I received a phone call to interview at Rutgers University. I left that day for the interview and returned the next evening. With the Toronado sold, we loaded the truck and started our long drive from Iowa to Delaware. We drove straight through. Both Carol and I were too full of anticipation, excitement, and optimism about the interview to sleep. I was told I would have an answer on Sunday regarding the position. I received a call from Dick Anderson, the Rutgers head coach offering me the job. Wow! What a relief and an opportunity! Coaching made little money at that time especially compared to today's salaries. So Carol found a job teaching school and commuted from Delaware to Princeton (a two-hour drive) for two months until we found housing.

At Rutgers, we had some big wins versus Penn State and Michigan State. But it was an uphill battle and the staff was fired after six years. It was in late November when we were let go and much like the last time I was unemployed, I spent days on the phone calling any school I thought had an opening. Most often I would leave a message for the appropriate coach or coaches and they would never be heard from again. There are few openings after February and most often none after March, except in very rare circumstances. My family had grown from two children to four with the addition of Bobby and Steve. More financial stress and pressure to land another job.

It was mid-February and I hadn't even had one phone call. My former college coach, Tubby Raymond, allowed me to volunteer at the University of Delaware. Carol was still teaching until the school year ended. If I didn't find work by then we were moving back with her parents. I would volunteer at Delaware and Carol would try to find a job as well, to save money on housing. In the meantime, I would make the hour and twenty-minute drive from our townhouse in Pennsylvania to the University of Delaware. Early in

March I was fortunate to land an interview at East Carolina University. It was a new staff with Head Coach Bill Lewis and a different staff from the one I had interviewed with six years prior. I felt the interview went well, but didn't hear any news for two to three weeks. I finally got the call and off we went to East Carolina University. Another fabulous opportunity to pursue my passion for coaching. This opportunity had me coaching outside linebackers. It was a low paying position so my wife Carol worked two jobs. She taught at a middle school and also worked as the head track coach for the university. With the cost of daycare, we barely made the monthly budget. I should say "rarely" made the monthly budget. But we had two wonderful years there.

My last year at East Carolina we won the Peach Bowl and Bill Lewis was a sought-after head coach. He took a job at Georgia Tech. Coach Lewis told me and the staff to go to the annual college coaching convention and he would contact us about who he would take to Georgia Tech. I went to the small airport to meet up with all the assistants leaving for the convention to find I was the only one there. My heart sank. I made a call and while I didn't get any concrete information, I had an idea I wouldn't be going to Georgia Tech.

I boarded a later flight to the convention and saw our training staff at a connecting city. They greeted me by saying, "Sorry to hear the news." "What news?" They of course felt terrible realizing I hadn't officially heard I wouldn't be going to Georgia Tech. Bill was apologetic about the miscommunication and asked if I would be interested in working with wide receivers. I thanked him for giving me the opportunity I had at East Carolina, but wanted to stay in my area of expertise which was on defense.

As it turned out, our offensive coordinator became the head coach and I became the defensive coordinator at East Carolina. I was on the job as defensive coordinator at East Carolina for a couple of months when Dave Wannstedt called wanting to meet me when he came to town to work out one of our top NFL prospects for the Dallas Cowboys.

We met in the hotel lobby and he asked if I would be interested in interviewing for the defensive assistant role with the Cowboys. Dave is very detailed and described in depth what the job would entail. He talked through the daily schedule and answered any questions I had. A couple of days later an interview was set up. I was to meet the staff at another one of the top NFL Draft workouts. Ironically, I met Jimmy Johnson and staff at Georgia Tech. I was offered the job and accepted with enthusiasm. I called my East Carolina head coach and told him of the opportunity. He was as excited as I was and wished me luck and gave me his blessing. Then I called Carol and asked her to pack enough of my clothes to last about a month and jumped on the private plane and finished the pro workout rounds before flying to Dallas and my new position.

A Coaching Life is full of detours, obstacles, new places and old places. It is exciting and disappointing. The winding road I traveled led me to a new and coveted career in the NFL!

A Coach's Life: The
Road From the Top

A FTER THE SUPER Bowl victory in 1993, Dave Wannstedt became the head coach of the Chicago Bears. He hired me as the defensive coordinator. It was a bold move considering I had been in the NFL for only one year and the Bears were known for great defense. Dave was a confident, detailed, and organized coach. He was also an outstanding defensive coordinator. I'm grateful for the confidence he displayed in me and the tremendous opportunity I was given.

Of all the head coaches I had the privilege to work for, Dave was the best leader and communicator. He had an ability, a charisma, and a presence to which the players could relate. He also had a belief in the staff as a unit. He hired people who not only had the expertise in their field, but people who would work well with others. Dave knew there was much more to being a great coach than X and O or technical knowledge. I spent six years with the Bears learning how to lead a defense and how to be led by a head coach.

I spent one very interesting year with the Cleveland Browns as the defensive coordinator. It was the expansion year and was very challenging. As the play caller, I felt I had to have the perfect call every play in order to succeed.

Leaving there after one year I joined the Green Bay Packers as the secondary coach. We had an excellent team with Brett Favre as the quarterback. We made the playoffs every year. I became the defensive coordinator my last year. We had a young defense and didn't meet the expectations of the head coach. He decided to make a defensive coordinator change. I then went to the Denver Broncos as the secondary coach. Mike Shanahan was head coach and a two-time Super Bowl winner with the Broncos. We were close to returning to the Super Bowl before losing the AFC Championship Game to the Pittsburgh Steelers. Mike Shanahan is fantastic at championing the cause for young coaches. He, more than any NFL head coach, has given opportunities to those who otherwise wouldn't have had many -- if any.

Two years later the staff was dismissed and I sat out one year before returning to the Washington Redskins as the secondary coach for two years and linebacker coach for two years to finish my NFL coaching career.

Those twenty years in the NFL as defensive coordinator and assistant coach were fascinating. I found inspiration everywhere: in my family, players I coached, coaches I admired. But we are human, we can lose focus. Sometimes we lose faith. I trust that if you take the time to give a good look around, you will find what you need to surmount obstacles.

I also believe we become a product of our own experiences. My spiritual foundation and my time in football have positively influenced the person I've become and helped me develop the proper mindset to navigate life's daily struggles.

LIFE AND LESSONS

I HAVE SHARED a little about my life because I wanted you to get a sense of where I have been and how I've been influenced. The man I have become is a reflection of the people I've met. I call these "lessons" because that's what the following experiences have been for me.

From the greatest game in the world, I learned how people respond to situations on a world stage.

Perhaps you will find something in these stories and observations that will ignite a desire to accomplish a specific goal. Perhaps one will help you surmount an obstacle, or maybe you'll see *yourself* in the experience and celebrate the person *you've* become.

Whether we know one another or not, we share a journey. A life that is given to us – one full of seeking and finding.

I hope the following collection of stories will give you a glimpse into the life of athletes and coaches at the pinnacle of their profession. May they provide meaningful motivation to competitors of all kinds looking to gain their edge. To find joy in the journey.

My wish is that I successfully share these insights into the inner workings of the NFL. I hope to inspire, explain, teach, detail, illustrate, and comment on my experiences. May you learn to leave a positive leadership legacy with messages of hope, determination, and passion for anyone in the game of life.

LIFE IN THE LEAGUE

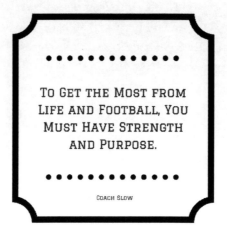

TO GET THE MOST FROM
LIFE AND FOOTBALL, YOU
MUST HAVE STRENGTH
AND PURPOSE.

COACH SLOW

Over my twenty years in the NFL, I crossed paths with players and coaches at the pinnacles of their careers. Many displayed the character-building traits that makes being part of a team so rewarding. They were hardworking, committed, passionate, relentless, determined, and persistent.

When the doors closed on my coaching career it didn't change my feelings about how fortunate I was to be part of such a popular game and more importantly, to work alongside such exceptional professionals.

So You Want To Coach Professional Football?

The in-season life of an assistant coach in the NFL is a pure grind as far as the time spent in the office preparing each week. Usually coaches will spend twelve-eighteen hours a day in the office. Most coaches are highly competitive. When their assigned tasks are completed and if there is still any fuel left in their usually depleted gas tank, they will find new ways to create more work for themselves to find an edge against the competition.

It seems coaches aren't satisfied until they feel they have completely exhausted themselves.

Most coaches were athletes themselves at some level so in order to make it through the insane hours and pressure, some coaches will find the early hours be-

CAROL AND OUR GRANDDAUGHTER, NATALIE

fore the grind begins to get a workout. Me being one of those coaches felt the workout (which was anywhere between thirty and sixty minutes) helped get my creative mind alert and active just before the day began. In my younger days, I would begin the workout at 6am at the facility. Depending on the commute that meant a 5am wake up at the latest. As I got into my last five or six years, for some reason this workout began earlier and earlier. My final three years started with a workout at 4-4:30am. My alarm was set for 3am (crazy!).

After the workout, the rest of your schedule varied somewhat from team to team or more accurately head coach to head coach or coordinator to coordinator.

In most organizations, there would be a staff meeting to begin the day with either the head coach or coordinator at 7am on Tuesday, Wednesday, Thursday, and Friday which are heavy work days. Monday varies because of travel or the time of Sunday's game. Saturdays are a walkthrough, travel, and evening meetings. Sunday is the normal Gameday.

On Tuesdays and Wednesdays, which are the heaviest days for workload, the day would normally end between 10pm and 12am. If you happened to be one of the early risers you could be talking about an eighteen-hour day easily. Thursday is a little shorter, ending anywhere from 5pm-8pm depending on your boss. Friday would end between 4-7pm and most coaches looked at it as their family or date night. From purely a total hour standpoint you can see it is not for the weak of heart or for those expecting to eat dinner at home or see their kids off to bed for seven to eight months of the year.

On top of what seems like endless hours, there is the stress that comes with the pressure of performing well at your position. If you happen to be short on talent or just don't meet the expectation level set by the head coach or coordinator, you can find yourself fired no matter how hard you've worked.

The ironic aspect of life in the league as an assistant coach is that it doesn't matter if you are winning or losing. The head coach is most certainly evaluated on wins and losses, but that is not the case for the position coach. It is one of the aspects about the league I believe is unfortunate because as much as it is a team game, this reality tears down the team building. Coaches with families have the added stress of leaving their home life to a single parent for seven months. Single coaches sacrifice social life or relationship building for seven months.

If you are looking for a job with high stress, long hours, insecurity, and regular relocations: then coaching professional football is right for you!

From College To The NFL

The last time I coached in the college ranks you played eleven or twelve regular season games and possibly a bowl game if invited. The regular season was over somewhere between Thanksgiving and the first week of December. You were allowed two weeks of pre-season practice before your opening regular season game.

After thirteen years of coaching in college I got my opportunity to coach in the NFL. It was 1992 and I was fortunate to join the Dallas Cowboys' coaching staff. Jimmy Johnson was the head coach and Dave Wannstedt, the defensive coordinator. Dave took me under his wing and helped me understand some of the differences between college and the league.

At that time, we had two weeks of training camp, then five pre-season games. Our first pre-season game was the American Bowl as it was called back then, held in Tokyo, Japan.

We spent the week in Tokyo practicing against what was then the Houston Oilers. Following that game, we played four more pre-season games. The training camp practices had no restrictions regarding contact: wearing pads or not wearing pads, or even how many practices per day. Bottom line, before we even played a regular season game we already went through the equivalent of half of a college season.

During this time, most teams left their normal team facility and went to a different location for training camp. So not only did you endure long sixteen-eighteen hour coaching days, but you were seven weeks away from home and family. We then began the sixteen-game regular season and its grueling coaching hours. Before we had even reached the halfway point in the regular season it was the equivalent of a full college season. Talk about going from a sprint to a marathon! I had already hit a wall at the end of training camp and was about to hit the wall again with eight games left in the regular season.

We finished the regular season winning our division and earning a bye for the first week of the playoffs. Coaches didn't get time off. We started our grind through game tape of potential opponents. We had a fabulous team and went on to win our three playoff games and become World Champions!

All in all, we had played twenty-four total games including pre-season. Basically, two college seasons with no break. So my first years as a professional coach would not only be gratifying earning a championship, but I must admit my first memories are of how long, exhausting, and grueling that first year as a professional was!

Another surprise to me as I reflect on that first year was how I could have been so far off in my impression of our team. It was difficult to see how great that team was because it was hard for anyone to stand out. In college, the range of talent is so much greater that good players easily stood out. When you had a half-dozen stand out players in college you assumed you would have a good team. I look back in awe of the talent Jimmy Johnson accumulated for the franchise.

THE MOST DIFFICULT COURSE YOU WILL EVER TAKE

Professional football players are, not surprisingly, phenomenal athletes. The speed and power displayed on the field is amazing even for a coach who has witnessed these feats for more than twenty years. Because of the length of the season and the violent collisions they must endure not just on game day, but in practice sessions, their durability is incredible.

To perform to the best of their ability they must be in top condition. As Vince Lombardi said, "Fatigue makes cowards of us all." Anyone who has played the game or any demanding sport will attest to that. A professional football playbook will easily contain 150 plays or more.

Until a player has been in the same system for at least a year, imagine being required to learn a new language and 150 different assignments in three weeks and then get thrown into battle every week to keep your job. Even though concepts in the game are mostly universal through the league, the languages are not. There is a learning curve to translate known concepts into a new language with a short turnaround time for take-off.

Not only are these players challenging themselves physically, but they are being pushed to the limit mentally as well. We have not even considered the emotional aspect of practice tedium and the constant stress of keeping your job.

An analogy of the game day test presented to a player would be to take a test on a subject matter that is demanding. But before being presented with your test question you must run fifty yards as fast as possible. After that sprint, you are given three seconds to answer. The test will have between sixty and ninety questions. You average about eighteen seconds before each question! Players earn their money!

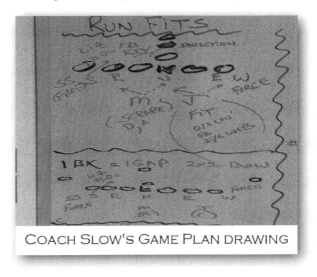

COACH SLOW'S GAME PLAN DRAWING

A MAN AND HIS WORK

The coaching life is not for anyone looking for security. Jobs are not only hard to come by, but difficult to keep as well. There's so much competition in the coaching field these days and there are so many intelligent, hard-working athletes aspiring to continue their careers as a coach. Professional football has opened its ranks to include women as well. Once you enter the career coaching world there are some tough realities you and your family will have to deal with.

There are only a few coaches who can start their career in the professional ranks. Most of these coaches are former NFL players who have prepared during their career by learning as much about the game and the coaching life as possible, as well as committing to being the best player possible. It is great to see some of these athletes who weren't the superstars of the sport find an opportunity in a career they so passionately embraced.

RYAN WITH TYE AND AVERIE
— THIS PUTS EVERYTHING BACK IN PERSPECTIVE

Regardless of how you get your chance, if you want to continue to climb the career ladder you will have to move, and move often.

I have coached thirty-five years and averaged a

move every three and a half years. I've known many coaches who have averaged moving every two years. For the coach, it can be an exciting time moving to a new team and a new adventure. The people who struggle the most are your wife and family. Finding a new place to live, trying to find new friends, and getting familiar and comfortable with the new area and staff members are only a few of the challenges. Often a new job means longer hours in the office, in the off-season, and even more time away from home because of it. A coach's wife is much like a single parent.

It is especially exciting when moving because of the promotion. More often than not, a coach will have to move because he has been fired and needs work. Sometimes the head coach is released and the staff with him. There are times the head coach fires a number of assistants. I've been through them all.

It is slightly easier when you have years remaining on your contract so you are guaranteed income to provide for your family as you seek a new job.

When your contract is up and you're fired, it is much more stressful.

The window to secure another job is small and the stress is compounded knowing a paycheck is soon going to end. I've been fired or searching for a job over half a dozen times. It is humbling and a real blow to your self-esteem when you are not nearly as sought-after as you may have thought. People who were interested in talking to you when you were coaching don't seem quite as interested any longer. When you walk around a crowd at the Senior Bowl or Scouting Combine it is like the Red Sea parting. People try to avoid speaking to you. You feel like you have a contagious disease.

You come to understand you have few, if any friends, but many acquaintances. I've been on both sides of the fence and think I've been very sensitive by talking to and helping if I could, someone looking for work. Simply returning a phone call, breaking the news that a job has been filled, or letting someone know you can't help is a professional courtesy lost on most people. Very few phone calls, emails or texts are ever responded to when you mention you are looking for a job.

It really does beat you down and can be difficult for the family to see their husband or dad face rejection after rejection and struggle to find work. There's a silver lining in these difficult times. If you keep your faith and stay strong displaying a kind and optimistic disposition, your wife and children gain a valuable life lesson. "God does not give us overcoming life; He gives us life as we overcome."[1]

One of my first times out of a job I was visiting my parents and grandparents in Pittsburgh and I was told something I'll never forget. My grandmother asked if I had found work yet. I told her I was still looking. She then responded with something simple and profound. She said, "A man is not a man without his work." OH, so true in so many ways!

THE MOST IMPORTANT TRAITS TO BE SUCCESSFUL IN THE NFL

Just like any other competitive career market you must possess a certain degree of talent. If I wanted to become a great mathematician but struggled to understand and master algebra in high school I probably don't have the aptitude, intelligence or let's say talent to attain that goal.

Professional football requires a certain degree of talent. If you lack the base level talent you will not make it in professional football regardless of having an abundance of other quality traits.

Any player making it to a professional football training camp has been studied and evaluated by coaches and scouts and deemed talented enough to be given a chance to prove themselves in training camp. From this point on let's assume everyone possesses enough talent.

What Are the Other Traits That Separate Players?

Next to talent I believe you must have a love and passion for the game and the process. Pro football is long, rigorous, and demanding physically, mentally, and emotionally. No matter how much allure the game offers in notoriety and money, without passion you will not succeed.

Not only must you love playing on Game Day you must enjoy the process of preparing:

- Professional football with its physical demands takes its toll on your body day after day.

- Professional football requires the same level of commitment in the classroom as it does on the field.
- Professional football players must learn and study the playbook, but must also put in extra time studying for their upcoming opponent.

The emotional toll is not often thought about. The majority of players are never secure in their job and carry the constant stress of being released at any time.

The daily grind of the same drills, study, and stress will wear on them if they don't love the game and its process. Passion and enthusiasm allow you to put yourself in motion, in action, effortlessly and easily without reluctance.

Players who treat their career as not only a job, but a discipline also have a greater chance of success. Much like the discipline of a martial artist, the professional football player must carry over his passion for the game and process into his personal life. This is done by taking care of himself with enough rest, diet, and discipline to refrain from the temptations that can derail his career regardless of how much he loves to play.

Another important trait the player must possess is mental toughness. There will be highs and lows, constant bumps, bruises and pain, criticism, and adulation. Through it all you must be mentally tough enough to prepare and play with the same competitive spirit. Talent plays a part, but attitude makes the difference in achieving success in professional football.

Fear

I am probably an expert in the area of fear and panic attacks. It is ironic that someone on the small side ends up coaching in the world of professional football with very large and intimidating athletes. Growing up being one of the small kids probably contributed to my constant anxiety, stress, and sometimes fear. It is difficult to have any joy when you are experiencing those emotions.

Fortunately, I had an older brother who was one of the bigger kids and best athletes in high school. He always took a very protective posture for his little brother. It probably kept me from being bullied. Which is and always has been an issue that is serious and real. I am grateful for my brother having my back, but until you can overcome your anxiety and fear on your own it will never be conquered.

I have the utmost empathy for anyone who is constantly living with fear. Somehow, I found a way to cope and battle through my own anxiety and fear. One tool for me was my daily scripture reading. Scripture states "Be Not Afraid" many times over and over. That alone helped me and my anxiety knowing that no matter what happened I would always be victorious in my faith!

I didn't play organized football until ninth grade and again had to overcome the fear of contact because I had never experienced it. Tackling drills were not organized by similar sizes. If it came to the smallest vs. the biggest, that was the luck of the draw. Surviving that on my own was one of the last steps of learning to overcome my fears and anxiety to build some self-esteem.

When I started coaching I never forgot what it was like to experience that fear for the physical aspect of the game -- which has become even more ferocious. It is extremely difficult for a player to reach their potential if they cannot overcome the aspect of fear.

When there is fear, there is no joy. If there is no joy, there is no real passion! I have been in many coaching staff meetings where players were belittled, berated, and overly criticized for being timid or fearful in the contact element of the game. Obviously as a coach, if a player lacks contact skills it is a liability in a collision sport.

As the level of competition increases from high school to professional football, non-contact players are slowly weeded out. Professional football still has players who don't like the contact, but possess other superior characteristics.

Knowing what it is like to overcome and cope with my own anxieties and fear has given me a different perspective than most coaches. Rather than belittle and degrade a person's fear, I applaud their great courage. It takes bravery to step on the field day after day and to overcome that fear and perform. What courage it takes for a young person to go to school every day and overcome the fear of seeing the bully.

Since the door closed on my professional coaching career I have expanded my horizons and went out of my comfort zone to grow and continue to overcome my own anxieties.

One of the most rewarding is starting to practice Gracie Jiu Jitsu with Coach Carlos Diaz in Destin, Florida. The Gracie program also offers a program called Bully Proof. It is one of my favorites because it gives the individual the tools and self-esteem and confidence to overcome fears. I empathize and hope everyone, especially young people living in fear, find their way to Be Not Afraid and overcome!

DO PROFESSIONAL PLAYERS GET NERVOUS BEFORE A GAME?

Much like professionals in any career from singers, dancers, comedians, entertainers, or actors and actresses, almost everyone experiences nervousness. Some more than others. Any business professional or someone in the military will have some nerves or anxiety when the time comes to put their training to use. The more prepared one feels, the less anxiety and nervousness you usually have.

Being well prepared and confident doesn't eliminate the nerves but will usually lessen the degree.[2]

Pro football players are no different regardless of their age or experience. The week builds through meetings and practice, thinking and action to prepare for the game. The fact that you move from training to the game and you have nowhere to hide in a full stadium does initiate some nervousness. Football players are similar to those serving in our military and their anxieties. Rarely does football have fatal consequences as in the military. The life or death consequences of a mistake in the military creates a higher level of stress. Both worlds are similar in the team aspect of the job. The professional players will stress most about failure and the possibility he could let his teammates down much like a soldier stressing over letting his fellow soldiers down. Even one mistake in an otherwise perfect performance could affect the entire outcome of the game.

Each and every team's goal is the same -- to be World Champs. With so much time, energy, sweat, and blood put into the preparation, the players are extremely sensitive to doing well for the team. It is not uncommon for them to wear their emotions on their sleeves. For some, with that much time shared in the grind of training, a bond is developed among the players. The stronger the bond, the better the team performs.

Preparing well doesn't guarantee victory because there are times that talent level or the game plans presented to the player are not adequate. I have seen over the years many players throw up in the locker room or on the field just prior to the game from nerves. Once they take the field their training kicks in and the nerves usually disappear. The anticipation of the competition creates the worst stress.

There are also times during the game when you may see an athlete appear nervous or stressed all of a sudden. This will happen to some players when it is known to all watching or competing that the outcome will be determined by the next play or plays. Players who allow their training and confidence to dominate their thoughts usually perform the best.

Yes, professional players get nervous mainly because they don't want to let their teammates down! In the back of their mind is the possibility of injury and the fact that their financial livelihood and career is based on their game day performance. Regardless of how well they train, they must produce on Game Day to keep their jobs!

NFL Players Have Beaten the Odds

Players who have made it to the NFL have beaten the odds. It requires an enormous base level talent to reach the NFL.

- Only 6.5% of high school players make it to the NCAA.
- Only 1.6% of NCAA players make it to the NFL.
- That translates to just under two players out of 100 draft-eligible NCAA football players.
- On average, there will be 300 rookies making a team yearly.
- One of the most startling facts about the NFL is that only 150 of all NFL players each year ever reach year four!

It is important that those football players fortunate enough to make it to the NCAA level, understand the odds of becoming an NFL player.

By no means should understanding the odds deter anyone from chasing their dream if that is their goal.

These incredible odds should help those aspiring NFL players realize they will have to have more than just talent to move to the pinnacle of their profession. Excelling not only on the field, but in the classroom as well.

Know your position, but also have a clear understanding of the other positions and how they relate to you. Be not only a great teammate but a leader as well. These are areas outside of talent that can help you reach the next level.

You would think the players who make it to the NFL and beyond four years have a certain degree of security. In most cases, even with the great players I have found a certain degree of insecurity. Not lacking confidence in any way, but an understanding there is always someone out there who could possibly take their job if they became complacent or comfortable.

More often than not great players are the most consistent, hardest working, best conditioned players on the team. They are also extremely reluctant to miss practice or games. The small degree of insecurity helps the players maintain their edge.

PRACTICE INTENSITY

The practices in professional football can vary according to the level of intensity and equipment worn. The base level of practices are walk-throughs. The practice is exactly as its name implies. Players do not wear shoulder pads or helmets. Players will dress in workout gear with their practice jersey on. Their practice jersey does correspond to their game jersey with the same number. In a walk-through session, the players will walk-through new plays and the daily install meeting they just heard in the classroom.

Normally the offensive and defensive units work separately. The normal format is to hear the information in the classroom first, walk-through the plays, then practice at game speed, followed by the game itself on Sunday. After the walk-through, teams will then practice the plays full speed. Full speed practice can be with different degrees of dress. Workout gear, shoulder pads, game jersey and helmet another level. Full pads is the most intense level which mimics a game with the exception of tackling teammates to the ground.

Once you pass the walk-through stage all other levels are full speed. The amount of contact and intensity of the contact is what coaches manage. It's important to have enough contact in preparation to feel confident and comfortable game day. It is also important to be safe so you can have your best lineup available game day. Don't have so much contact that players are getting hurt in practice, or over a period of time lose their crisp, hard-hitting hunger. Injuries can never be completely controlled but must be a primary concern. All teams want the best players playing. The level of intensity at practice is designed for the most efficient progression for learning and staying healthy.

Professional football differs greatly from college in that pro players can practice any level of intensity with very few athletes ever hitting the ground. In college football, you will see more players getting off the ground. Part of the reason is the fact college athletes as a whole are not nearly as talented; and also, pro players have learned how to practice with great intensity yet keep each other off the ground.

When players are going to the ground the risk of injury is much greater. The coach must find the right balance of contact and non-contact to be prepared and stay healthy.

LOUD COACHING

Every coach, just like every person, has their own unique personality. In my thirty-five years of coaching I've worked for many different head coaches. I've also had the opportunity as a defensive coordinator to observe position coaches on the field and in the classroom.

My personality and background is that of an educator or teacher. Most likely it came from my experience when I was playing football at the University of Delaware. The coaches were all organized, passionate, and prided themselves as teachers. We didn't have what I would consider really loud coaches. The loud coach is not one who is loud only by volume but also by his vulgar, demeaning, and negative style. There are leaders in football and other professions who prefer this loud and intimidating approach. I've been on many staffs where the head coach also prefers and encourages this style of coaching. It can be very effective as well.

When that is your methodology, usually it is a result of a lack of confidence in your knowledge, organization, communication, or teaching.

My preference has always been more of the teaching or educator's approach. I do think it has slowed me down in my professional advancement. It is important for leaders to be sure they are not mistaking kindness for weakness.

Loud doesn't always mean strong, demanding, detailed, and organized. There are times loud in volume is necessary; and it's even more effective when it is used sparingly.

Words that build up, encourage, and inspire players will benefit more in the long run. There are many scripture quotes about the benefits of building others up. ".... authority the Lord gave me for building up and not for tearing down." (2 Corinthians 13:10)

Free Agent Fallacy

Free Agency has changed professional football in a number of ways. No longer can you assume your favorite player or the team's best player will remain with that organization any longer than their contract length. It has also leveled the playing field where teams that are struggling can become competitive very quickly by good choices in the draft and free agency. In this era of free agency, dynasties are difficult. It takes a great organization to sustain championship level play and talent.

I have witnessed many coaches and leaders fall prey to the thinking that a high profile, popular, highly sought-after, and highly-priced player is best.

There have been times when that free agent, for various reasons, is just not a good fit to continue building towards a championship. It could be that your existing talent simply won't be good enough for that high dollar acquisition to be effective. It's possible your scheme and tactics don't suit this player as well. The media will initially welcome this kind of player with great fanfare, he will stir great interest. When the team falters or the free agent doesn't fulfill expectations that are unrealistic, he will become the primary target of criticism. This can easily become a distraction.

All of this can be avoided by one simple rule. Do your homework! There is absolutely no reason a team and an organization shouldn't know exactly what they are buying.

I have been with some organizations that sign a player as a free agent and pay a high price because the market dictates the value and think the player's on-field production will change to reflect the market. That is the number one fallacy. The player you sign will be the same player you viewed on the video. There may be small degrees of change for good or bad, but an organization that does its homework will not be surprised.

It is easier to manage the media's expectations by educating them and the fan base as to exactly what was bought.

It is amazing to me that in the NFL and its billion-dollar business, general managers, head coaches, and organizations will invest millions of dollars without being thorough in the evaluation process and investigating the move from all angles. There are teams that simply don't do their homework or ignore the data because of the initial excitement created for the team.

Many organizations fail because of their arrogance. With the popularity of professional football and technology with access to all games, new analytical companies have been born. They grade every single player on every single play. Because some of the analysts are not scouts or coaches, an organization's arrogance that anyone but themselves can grade a player prevents them from using a valuable tool to offset their own work.

THE FIRST 15

When you hear announcers or coaches talk about the "First 15" they are referring to the first fifteen plays the offense will run in the game. When the First 15 goes smoothly it will most likely end in points scored.

On a classic First 15 drive, the offense will use a variety of personnel groupings to keep the defense off balance and try to get them out of rhythm. The First 15 is fast-paced when the offense stays on schedule because it is already scripted and the play caller simply goes down his list. The offensive players are in tune because these fifteen plays were reviewed in detail the night before the game.

The offense not only changes personnel groupings, but also changes the complexion of the plays from play action pass, run, screens, draw, drop back, reverse or some other gadget.

The First 15 will try to test every aspect of your defense and that's why it is difficult to stop.

When the defense gets an early stop within the First 15 it is a great confidence boost; while it is a letdown for the offense because so much effort was put into choosing, practicing, reviewing, and scripting those plays to open the game.

Good defensive coaches separate and study the first fifteen plays of the game as a special category. It is important for the players to be prepared for a fast pace and a multitude of personnel and variety of plays to defend.

The First 15 has become a game within the game!

COACH SLOW'S LIST OF GAME WEEK
NICKEL PLAYS

THE COACHING CONUNDRUM

Coaches who have reached the highest level of their profession often find themselves in their own philosophical conundrum. Coaches by nature are normally very critical people, but having a critical eye is something all good coaches should possess. It is the coach's job after all to facilitate his players' improvement.

Without a keen eye for the details and techniques necessary for success -- that would pose an insurmountable problem. Being able to discern the element of a professional player's game that needs improvement is only the first part of coaching.

It is necessary to present these deficiencies in a way that inspires the player to an even greater level of performance. That can be the coaching conundrum.

The delivery of the evaluation is just as important as the content. The majority of coaches, even at the NFL level, emphasize the areas of the players' performance that needs improvement. Coaches have been conditioned throughout their coaching career to find the weaknesses in the opponent and in their own players.

Coaches have always believed if a performance is good it can be better. Therein lies the conundrum.

When your players are performing well yet are constantly bombarded by criticism of how they can be better, it will tear down the players' psyche. It can quickly breed a mentality that nothing will ever be good enough so why try to achieve anything that is not easy and comfortable.

A great coach can:

- Take the same performance to first, and most importantly, reinforce the positives.
- Filter in some of the weaknesses that can improve the performance slowly.
- Spread these out so as not to take away from the positive aspects.
- Explain the video of players performing the techniques and displaying competitive attitude you are trying to achieve.

This positive mental intermarry of the tasks you want performed are more likely to lead to that destination. Mental pictures of what not to do often leads to more negative actions.

Emphasizing the positive is not ignoring the elements that must be improved to attain all of your team goals. Team members must know you are honest in your evaluations. This leads to trust. Being honest in post-performance evaluations will help in game planning for your players' strengths.

Too many coaches spend an inordinate amount of time trying to fix a weakness rather than play to strengths. By playing to your team members' strengths it is a much smoother transition to address their weaknesses.

Great coaches utilize their team's talents best and inspire the players to improve their weaknesses.

THE NFL SCOUTING COMBINE: INSIDE THE PLAYER INTERVIEWS

I've been with six different NFL teams and have attended the Indianapolis Scouting Combine with all six teams to interview college prospects for the NFL Draft.

Every team is a little different with the interview procedure.

One year when I was the assistant head coach and defensive back coach with Green Bay, I was fortunate to sit in on every player interview. With all but one of the teams, the head coach sat in on every meeting. The General Manager, National Area Scout, and Director of Player Personnel were also in attendance. The respective coordinator and potential position coach handled the football Xs and Os aspect of the interview.

The normal procedure started with the general manager or scout gathering the prospect's general information such as agent and phone number. Occasionally they would ask about family just to get the prospect talking and comfortable. If there were any character issues or arrests, these items would also be addressed at that time. Most often these interviews are not like an interrogation, but a conversation. The head coaches and general managers usually have one or two questions to see if they can get a glimpse into what motivates the prospect and makes him tick.

One of my favorite head coach questions was when Mike Sherman, the head coach of the Green Bay Packers at the time, would ask the prospect if they had ever had a job. He would also ask if they ever missed work and why. Prospects who had jobs were used to working. Prospects who were reliable in those low-level positions were more likely to be reliable in the high-profile NFL.

Prospects who never had a real job may not understand the mentality of the NFL.

PLAYING HURT

NFL players are extremely competitive and are also very tough both mentally and physically. Football is a high impact collision sport. NFL practices are also very intense even when they are non-contact. When viewing a game or practice from the sideline there is an obvious sense of extraordinary speed. The NFL game is much faster and more explosive than one can imagine.

Players can react in an instant and change direction on a dime. These types of explosive movements take their toll on one's body over time. As players work through training camp into the regular season there is not a player who is not sore or in pain. Playing through soreness and pain is part of the job outside of the glamour, notoriety, and money. The bumps and bruises are normal much like any of us working through the soreness of yesterday's workout.

Injured players are not the same. Injured players are those who have an injury diagnosed by the trainer or medical staff. There are degrees of injuries from strains and sprains to broken bones. It is the medical staff's job to determine if the player has enough strength and mobility to play safely in the game without causing more damage.

Contrary to what you might think, it is usually the player who refuses to miss practice time or a game. The training and medical staff are normally quite conservative in the prognosis of returning the athlete to the field.

The NFL Concussion Protocol must be followed before a player can return to competition. Returning to competition for injuries outside of the concussion protocol is decided by the trainers, players, and coaches. Players are competitive, tough, and like soldiers. They are warriors who, like the competition, do not want to let their team and team members down. Most great players also have a degree of insecurity and do not want their teammate who will be taking their snaps, also taking their job. It is for these reasons players will compete even when feeling less than 100%.

In my twenty-year coaching career in the NFL, there were more occasions than I can count of a player begging trainers and coaches to play. Even the great players who give a valiant effort and play through pain are not as productive as their back-up would have been playing at 100%. Some of you may have seen players with one hand or the other bandaged into a large ball with no use of their fingers. I am certain you are not an effective player with the use of only one hand no matter how talented, compared to a player who can use two hands. Lower body injuries fall into the same category. If you are not at full speed you should not be on the field.

Players who play with injuries not only hurt themselves, but hurt their team as well.

I would urge all coaches to keep their injured players off the field no matter how convincing their sales pitch. Return them to the field only when they are fully recovered for their sake and the team's.

ONE MOMENT AT A TIME

Life is a lot like football and football is a lot like life. It's a finite period of time -- an opportunity, a chance to do the best job you can. To get the most out of life or football you must immerse yourself in the action. Get in the game.

To succeed at football and any sport you must play one play at a time. To be successful in the game of life you must be present in each and every moment as often as possible. Competing in this way whether in sports or in life is easier said than done.

When competing on the field, players are constantly bombarded with external and internal factors that distract their focus from the play. The score of the game can distract us from our focus. When you are behind, it is easy to let negative energy affect your field disposition, body language, and concentration. When you or your team is way behind on the scoreboard there is a tendency to lose hope, and give up against what appear to be too great of odds.

The same factors can affect us in our daily lives. Circumstances in life's daily battles can distract us from our

ME AND RYAN ON A GAME DAY MORNING

family, relationships, and job. Guard against letting the valleys in the daily journey of living prevent us from being positive, conscientious, caring, and respectful. Continue to forge ahead toward fulfillment.

There are times in football games when your team is way ahead and the urge is to let up. Champions fight that urge and play a single play at a time with effort, energy, enthusiasm, focus, and execution of the smallest details; regardless of the score.

When things are going well in life's journey it's easy to let up on the spiritual foundation that got you to your place of fulfillment.

Coaches are constantly preaching to players: "Don't let one poor play turn into three or four."

This occurs when a player can't let go of the previous poor play. He then lacks the focus, concentration, and attitude necessary to execute the technique and play properly, resulting in another poor play. Players must learn to have a short memory. Oftentimes, coaches perpetuate this cycle themselves by reviewing the game with constant emphasis on the negative. By doing this, players are more likely to hang on to their mistakes.

Life is similar. It is easy to hang on to negative experiences which prevent you from growing and finding the positive possibilities right in front of you.

Prisoners of the Past
In Gary Barnett's book, *High Hopes*, I read about a story of hunters who found a humane way to capture exotic monkeys.[4] They first discovered that monkeys love cookies. They then built heavy boxes with a hole cut on each side, just large enough for the monkey's open hand to squeeze through. They placed cookies inside and left to return hours later.

What they later discovered was at least one monkey sitting alongside each box, every one with a hand stuck inside. The monkeys had grabbed the cookies so tightly, but wouldn't let go, so they couldn't remove their hands. They chose to hold on to the cookie, and become a prisoner instead.

The lesson of course is we must let go of the past to grow and move forward in football and in life. Scripture teaches the same lesson stating, ".... any man who puts his hand to the plow and looks back is not fit for service in the kingdom." (Luke 9:2)

TEAM BUILDING ACTIVITIES

Many of the head coaches I've coached planned some off-field activities instead of a practice to give the team members a mental and physical break from training camp, but also to try to bring the team together on a personal competitive level, outside of football. The different activities the head coaches chose were interesting alone. The best plan was carried out in Green Bay.

The team was on the practice field just finishing warm-up when five buses pulled up close to the locker rooms. Like everyone else, I couldn't help but notice them and wonder what they were for. Then the air horn blew twice indicating it was time to gather up with the head coach. Training Camp practices in Green Bay were almost always open to the public. There happened to be a large crowd that day. The head coach instructed players to head back to the locker room for further direction. We were all puzzled.

When we arrived at our lockers, there were instructions to put on the directed attire and load the buses. The beauty of the plan was the secrecy and starting in practice uniform on the field first.

THE MEN OF MY FAMILY
(L TO R: BOBBY, ME, RYAN, STEVE, AND TYE IN THE FRONT ROW)

It was an exceptionally hot and humid day. The head coach's direction to head to the locker room was met with a tremendous roar. The deception was flawless. Not only were the players and coaches duped, but so were the fans. I don't think they were as enthusiastic as the team was about practice ending after 15 minutes! The head coach carried out the deception like a well-designed game plan.

Back to the different activities. The most popular choice by head coaches was bowling. Normally it was set up with a competitive format. Offense vs. Defense as an example. I don't think of bowling as an activity based on the team building aspect as much as it was the easiest logistically with a confined area and a ready-made kitchen for food and drinks. Softball was another activity which worked well logistically and was thoroughly enjoyed by players and staff. A minor league venue made it accessible and convenient. We had one attempt at golf with one organization. It was not a disaster, but I wouldn't recommend it. The players were challenged by the game with the exception of most quarterbacks and kickers.

Getting back to the Green Bay activity. We were instructed to dress in sweatshirts and sweatpants and wear our gloves like receivers; all of that was very strange considering it was 88° and the humidity was around 90%. The buses loaded and off we went. Twenty minutes into the trip there was not a house or business within miles, we were somewhere in the middle of rural, wooded Wisconsin landscape. A minute or two later we turned onto a dirt road and stopped near a clearing about a half mile in. As we unloaded, we each grabbed two bottles of water and walked a quarter mile to the clearing. There we found two wooden towers and a dozen or more people handing out protective headgear and weapons. We were going to paint-ball war!!! Offense vs. Defense.

Game plans were made on the fly. Whoever captured the opponent's tower first was the winner. Plays were made, leaders emerged, and the battle began. Chaos ensued. Getting hit by a paintball is not pleasant and almost everyone had the welts to prove it. What a day! It was just as sweaty a workout in those pants and long sleeves as a practice. It was also by far the best kept secret and most fascinating of all the team building activities I've experienced.

DRAFT SETBACKS AND SURPRISES

Once teams venture into the month of June the draft has come and gone. The months of work put in by the coaches studying, interviewing, and writing evaluations of potential picks have played out on the practice field. The scouts' investment into talent acquisition has now transitioned to practice field evaluations. Coaches and scouts watch the rookies intently as they evaluate every aspect of their game on the field and off. It has however, somewhat baffled me that there are setbacks with some top choices and surprises with some players who were late round picks or college free agents. As I pondered the reasons for this it compelled me to review the evaluation process and its evolution over the years.

The NFL Scouting Combine has always been one of the major steps in evaluating prospects apart from viewing and grading players on their game video. The next step twenty years ago was to have position coaches go to the prospect's campus for a private workout. This method was completely unique to each team: how long the workout lasted, the drills and interview process, and film viewing.

Some of the projected first to third round picks may have workouts scheduled every day of the week for a number of weeks. This would take its toll physically on the player. Most players now only workout at the combine and on the school's designated pro day. Occasionally there may be private workouts for the top twenty picks.

Private workouts are not merely important for evaluating a player's physical skill, but also to evaluate a prospect's work-related interest and endurance. The benefit of the college campus visit and workout went well beyond the physical aspect. Teams are now using sophisticated and expensive psychological and personality profiling testing to project an athlete's success. These test results are interesting, but they cannot replace a position coach's opportunity to spend a full day with an athlete evaluating every aspect of the prospect's work mind and heart.

A typical schedule would include meeting for breakfast, viewing a weight room session, coaching the players through specific movements and techniques on the field, having lunch, and finally spending two to three hours viewing video and grinding through a board session.

After spending a full day with a potential acquisition in this manner, there are few questions that go unanswered. These on-campus private workouts have become few and far between. I absolutely loved those times and it was certainly revealing as to whether the prospect loved it as well. What you'd learn:

- Will the position coach and player have the proper chemistry?
- Does the player grasp new board strategy or field techniques quickly?
- Does the player have the baseline football knowledge to easily transition to the pros?
- Will his personality mesh with the position group?
- Will he be a team player?
- Does the player have the endurance, focus, and passion to maintain interest through a tough workday?

These questions are more easily answered through these personal workouts. No single test is a substitute for this. Why are there setbacks and surprises? The shift away from the personal workouts is one reason.

The Battle vs. Game Day Elements

When watching a professional football game at any level, it is perceived as one team pitted against another; one team in a battle against their opponent.

There is an underlying psychology when a team takes the mental approach they are playing their opponent. That immediately gives the opponent credibility as a formidable foe. I have preached often to players that we are not playing them; they are playing us. By planting that seed I was trying to give our players a boost of confidence or self-esteem.

I would like to do this especially versus an opponent that was close in talent or even slightly more talented to eliminate any self-doubt. It was also a way to bring the emphasis back on executing our techniques and knowing our assignments. By having few mental errors and taking pride in doing the fundamentals with great technique and detail, it would give us the best chance to win.

When a team emphasizes what an opponent does and how to anticipate their actions, tactics, and strategies, it is easy to lose its own identity of play execution. When this occurs, the post-game analysis is usually one of missed assignments, poor techniques, and poor tackling. The preparation must be a balance of execution and anticipation based off education.

Many fans view football on television rather than in person. Some aspect of the battle is lost because it is difficult at times when watching from the comfort of your home or the local sports bar to grasp the battle that goes on versus the elements.

Wind, rain, heat, cold, and field conditions are things to which television doesn't do justice.

We are accustomed to video games and their realistic features so we sometimes forget these are real circumstances the players are dealing with and are not in the least bit immune to.

Wind is not a factor for defensive players or offensive lineman, but affects quarterbacks and pass catchers as well as kickers, punters, and punt returners. It is much more difficult to throw accurately and to catch when the ball moves like a baseball pitch.

The heat is an element every player on the field must deal with. It can be as much a mental toughness battle as a physical challenge. The heat can be dangerous and all the players are watched closely by trainers and medical personnel.

The cold is just simply uncomfortable and makes the collisions much more painful. The body is just not as supple and loose. Catching a pass can be painful to the hands.

A wet, sloppy, or slippery field is extremely frustrating for the defense. Defensive players must react and find themselves much slower to execute their assignment. The advantage of a great take-off on pass downs is negated.

The elements are a real factor in a game outcome that is lost in the broadcast and can only be fully appreciated if you are out there in the elements as well.

LEADERSHIP LEGACY

AUTHENTIC LEADERS BESTOW
FEELINGS OF "GREATNESS" –
THEY DON'T TAKE THEM.

COACH SLOW

I held several coaching positions in the NFL, but never that of a head coach. I have been a defensive coordinator with the responsibility of leading not only the defensive staff, but the defense as a unit. I have also been a position coach. These roles gave me the unique perspective of what it takes to lead and how to be effective as a team member being led.

That perspective taught me a great deal about human nature, especially when it was on display beneath the bright lights of a stadium.

Over all those years and all those games, I've found that a man, through determined preparation and an extraordinary belief can achieve heights never imagined. It is also true that the most successful coaches can sell their team on the concept that in order to achieve greatness, they must forget greatness.

AUTHENTIC LEADERS

The most effective and productive leaders of team-related ventures have a chemistry or charisma with their team. It begins with trust. Trust begins with honesty and a vision for the team. The leader casts a vision and the foot soldiers carry out the plan. Communication is critical to the process.

ME AND MY BEST FRIEND, CAROL

It is important the leader conveys his vision clearly and thoroughly to his lieutenants who will then make sure all team members have a clear view of the destination. Along the journey there will be twists and turns and ups and downs. The leader must continually update the team with any adjustments in the course along the journey. He must be sure to reiterate that the destination is the same.

Although his top assistants will have the most contact with team members, the leader or head coach in professional football will meet regularly with the team to reinforce his vision and the steps necessary to reach the top. All teams and organizations will suffer setbacks, bumps in the road, injuries and all sorts of adversity and distraction. Those leaders that can convince their team they are temporary and every setback has a lesson to be learned have the greatest success.

I have seen the leaders who are on a mission to convince the team members and organization of their own greatness. These are the pseudo leaders looking for more money, notoriety, brand building, and power to satisfy their egos.

The authentic leader on the other hand because of the honesty, caring, common goal, chemistry, charisma, and clarity of the vision convinces the team of their greatness. These are the leaders of Champions.

DEVELOPING YOUR COACHING PHILOSOPHY

It is important that every coach and leader establish for themselves a personal leadership philosophy that they believe in. I'm not speaking of simply strategy and tactics, but rather the core of your moral fiber and what it is that drives your passion.

There are many types of management styles, all of which have seen success. A personal leadership philosophy and the management style that might live with it can be easily found by your motivation to succeed. Sometimes motivation for success is purposely driven by self-serving rewards such as money, notoriety, power, celebrity status, cars, homes and brand building.

When you are driven by those rewards it is easy to coach and lead with the end result: bottom line and wins and losses as your only necessary measuring stick for success. It is easy to ride the roller coaster of emotion and make decisions with no concern for your team members. A heavy hand of power brings some short-lived gratification to fulfill your desire and motivation to succeed.

My own personal coaching philosophy stems from two sources. The first is a scripture verse, I Thessalonians 3:12-13, "May the Master pour on the love so it fills your lives and splashes over on everyone around you, just as it does from us to you. May you be infused with strength and purity, filled with confidence..."

In whatever role I had, my primary motivation was to help those I coached move closer to their potential, not only as players but as men. Making the small world I worked and lived in better in some way brought me satisfaction and joy. Stressing the fact that as we strive to become the best we will face adversity, setbacks, and successes. It will be the process (specific action steps) of striving to become the best and the journey along the way from which we will achieve the most growth and reward.

Coaches and Leaders should be responsible for more than just wielding their power. I've thought of leadership this way. Which will have the greater result? To impose one's will upon another to act, or to inspire another to act upon his will? There will be many times coaches or leaders will be required by circumstance to be the boss and wield that power, but great leaders are not consumed and corrupted by the power itself.

The other source that describes my personal philosophy is from the book *The Teachings of Don Juan* by Carlos Castenada, "Look at every path closely and deliberately. Try it as many times as you think necessary. Then ask yourself and yourself alone the question.... does this path have a heart? If it does, the path is good. If it does not it is of no use."[3]

Hopefully more coaches and leaders will develop their own personal leadership philosophy based on not only winning, but building future leaders and coaches we would all aspire to be led by.

COACHING IS MORE THAN X & O KNOWLEDGE

When coaches and scouts evaluate players, it is common to consider the measurables of height, weight, speed, and position-specific movements as the prospect's talent level. A player's talent level is only one factor in determining the player's future success. Hard work, persistence, determination, and passion are just a few of the other ingredients required to succeed to the pinnacle of one's profession. Just as it requires more than talent to become a successful player, it takes more than Xs and Os to become a successful coach. "I've never seen that coach make a tackle or catch a pass." Coaches, coach; Players, play!

> *Coaching is unlocking a person's potential to maximize their growth.*[5]
> - John Whitmore.

It's not how much a coach knows, but how much he can teach his team members for useful application and competition.

- The best coaches are organized and passionate about educating their players or team members.
- The best coaches refine and discipline specific actions that are critical to winning.

The game of football requires an ability to quickly diagnose moving parts in a lightning fast landscape. Material is first presented in the low stress environment of the classroom. The speed for which they need to know is increased, and then put together for stress and speed on the practice field, and finally taken to the game. Educating players on the situational components of competition is often neglected by the average coach. Well coached position and team players execute great situational football.

Knowledge of Xs and Os is a critical part of coaching, but teaching the Xs and Os is also integral in the final product.

MY SON BOBBY, OUR GRANDDAUGHTER, NATALIE, AND LUCY

IT'S A PRIVILEGE TO COACH IN THE NFL

My time coaching in the NFL was rewarding, challenging, stressful, exhilarating, and also a privilege. The first time I put on gear that carried the NFL shield was exciting. The idea I was having an opportunity to be part of a world of coaches and athletes at the pinnacle of their profession was stimulating and intoxicating. I couldn't stop peeking at that shield every time I would put on a different piece of clothing. I would think, "Wow! I'm really here coaching."

It's more than the fact the league is so popular, but the people in the league are so special. I reflect on my career and the years I spent coaching in the league and feel proud -- from winning a championship to coaching on an expansion team with one win. I enjoyed being part of an elite group of athletes and coaches.

So many of the players and coaches display the character-building traits that makes being part of a team so rewarding: hardworking, committed, passionate, relentless, determined, and persistent to name a few.

When the doors closed on my professional coaching career it didn't change my feelings about how fortunate I was to be part of such a popular game and more importantly, so many exceptional people.

SUCCESSFUL LEADERSHIP METHODS

Throughout my professional and college coaching career I have witnessed and experienced firsthand, many different successful leadership methods. Micro-managing, loud and boisterous, arrogant and unapproachable, combative and obsessive to name a few, are some of the negative methods that have worked. Unfortunately, these methods are sometimes attractive to those who live in the world of instant gratification and pander to the hard-handed, "success now or be fired" approach.

From the outside, these approaches make the leader appear tough and powerful. There are certainly times when changes need to be made.

Authentic Leaders Don't Take These Decisions Lightly

A leader who constantly makes changes on his staff might have forgotten the impact the changes have on the human level of wives and families. He should also look at his own hiring process if he is making that many mistakes. When leaders put the passion into hiring their staff and have confidence in their decisions, it's important to give the staff the necessary time to teach, coach, and inspire the players on the journey. It takes both talent and leadership to win. You would not win one without the other.

Authentic leaders trust the plan, adjust when necessary, embrace the journey, develop future leaders, strive and die to their goal, but continually increase the quality of their team's life as well. It's a delicate balance that can only be achieved through an authentic leader's mentality. Authentic leaders understand that once one goal has been achieved there is another waiting.

Therefore, the journey, the process and relationships along the narrow road and difficult way, is the real game.

- Keep your team engaged and invested in the journey
- Acknowledge every success along the path
- Use each setback as a lesson from which to learn
- Have the confidence in yourself as a leader to allow input from your team to keep everyone involved and create a sense of ownership in the process

Winning the Championship is the ultimate goal for an authentic leader. Understanding that it is in the doing, not what has been done that leads to a championship mindset.

The Book of Proverbs states: "There is one who makes himself rich yet has nothing, and one who makes himself poor and comes to great riches." In other words, one says "look what I have done!" and ends up with nothing but themselves and one who keeps on giving no matter the cost and comes to great riches.

Develop a championship mindset that will bring great riches. Riches meaning joy, satisfaction, and peace in the doing. "Be strong and of good courage for there is reward for your work." (Chronicles 15:7)

Authentic leaders who understand the real game is not always wins and losses or the bottom line on a spreadsheet, will not only win championships, but are champions in the process!

DESTINATION

As the leader of your team, it is vital you provide a vision for the destination. In order to cast a vision, you must address your team or organization shortly after you have accepted your leadership position. Do not however cast a vision that is not complete or for which you were not thoroughly prepared.

It is also wise for the leaders of each segment of the team to present the vision they have for their team's role in the organization's destination. Each of these coaches should think of themselves as the head coach of their position. The message delivered by the lieutenants or position coaches should be clearly reinforcing the head coach's vision. Leaders cast a vision, but it is the foot soldiers who guarantee the outcome.

I have been on teams where the head coaches speak to the team every day of the week. I was on one team where the head coach spoke to the team only a few times per week and even that was not a certainty.

As one of the coaches who is also a member of the audience listening to the head coach's or leader's message, I do have an opinion.

MY YOUNGEST SON, STEVE ENJOYING THE BEACH

The coach who made the biggest impression and had the most sticky or easy to remember message was the coach who spoke only when he felt he had an important message to deliver.

When the team was addressed daily it wasn't too long before the noise started to drown out the vision.

Noise being distraction, lack of attention, and simply listening to the same voice every day. When the head coach addressed the team at different times it carried a much different connotation. The team immediately had a sense that what the head coach was about to say was significant and important. When the head coach addresses the team daily, it simply becomes part of the weekly routine. So, the message becomes routine. On the days the head coach does not speak, it also gives the coordinators a more powerful platform for their presentation as well.

As you and your team journey towards your destination, it is the coach's job to provide direction and to keep the vision in clear sight. As you do this, keep your meetings powerful and impactful by addressing your team when necessary rather than just as a normal part of a routine.

WHY GAME DAY MINDSET?

I don't proclaim to be a life coach. I'm not a sports psychologist. I'm a football coach.

As a coach, I've done my best to educate and teach young men fundamentals, tactics, and strategies of the game to help them reach their potential. As a coach, I've also done my best to present a message to the players just before competition that I hoped would help them have the proper mindset for that particular circumstance.

Circumstances that apply not only to that game, but to the game of life as well. I've always thought the message needed to be brief. As players get closer to kick off, the attention span for words and talk becomes shorter. A concise message helps bring out the inner fire they already have. Fanning the flame was my desire.

This was one of my favorite times with my players. It is a time when their emotions can be seen simmering on their skin. I hope I've inspired a few and I'm sure many were uninspired. Making the effort to me was important. Have a Passion for Good and Do Good with a Passion!

If a game day mindset message helped even one player it was worth it. That one player may be the one who wins the game for the team.

I've not always been one to look for good but now more than ever, you will find what you look for. If you keep looking for good you will find it.

COACHING CAN MAKE A DIFFERENCE

Whatever level you happen to be working at, you can make a difference. Coaching in professional football is the secret ingredient to success. I'm not speaking of the head coach only, but of all the coaches on the staff.

The talent level of professional players is so close that other factors become increasingly important. Coaches spend the most time with the players refining and disciplining specific actions that are critical to winning. A team may have more talent than any other team in the league, but without the proper coaching could wind up with a mediocre season.

LEARNING FROM THE BEST.
ME WITH THREE OF GRACIE JIU-JITSU'S FINEST
(L. TO R. RYRON GRACIE, ME THE STUDENT, CARLOS DIAZ, AND EVANDRO NUNES)

The strategy and tactics utilized by each team is one way to gain an advantage. These strategies normally run from the top down. The individual tactics and techniques specific to positions are the primary responsibility of the position coach. Position coaches have a unique opportunity to not only impact the physical aspect of their players' performance, but also the mental and emotional aspect of the game as well.

There are some coaches who ignore that element of educating their players. Those coaches believe it's the sole responsibility of the individual to be mentally and emotionally prepared.

My belief is that no matter what your age or experience, a little inspiration and education to help fan the flame is beneficial. It surely doesn't hurt, but could help. Preparing the players in every possible area that affects performance is prudent.

Talent plays a part, Xs and Os play a part, but attitude can make the difference!

THE ELUSIVE 100%

Coaches and leaders in any capacity work tirelessly to inspire their team members to give 100% in their role. It is important the coach and leader know exactly what they're asking for in demanding 100%. The most important aspect of 100% is the fact that by 100% we're speaking of 100% effort.

A person is born and blessed with a certain degree of talent which is beyond their control. Strategies and tactics are filtered down the chain of command for application in competition by competitors on the field of battle. Team members at times have input into the strategies and tactics. This will vary from coach to coach and leader to leader. Each of us, regardless of our role, has sole control over the amount of effort we put into our work.

What then does a 100% effort actually entail? I believe you must first be certain you acquire team members who will treat their job and role as a mission. A mission is defined as an operation or task assigned by a higher authority. "Whatever you do, work at it with all your heart, as for working for the Lord, not for men, since you know you will receive an inheritance from the Lord as a reward." (Colossians 3:23-24)

With that in mind, a 100% effort means using every fiber of body, mind, and soul to complete your mission:

- You are training properly and taking care of your body.
- You are continuing the education needed to perform your task.

- You are refining and disciplining the specific actions necessary to succeed in your role.
- You stay positive in all of your work circumstances and maintain a pleasant disposition to your teammates or anyone you interact with on task.
- You accept responsibility for attaining your goals.
- You understand that anything worthwhile is never the easy road. It is always the hard road.
- You also understand that this road is less traveled and it is on the journey itself you work to acquire fulfillment!

Most of us, even at the pinnacle of our profession, cannot honestly say we give a 100% effort all the time. Those who do take the road less traveled of 100% effort are most certainly on their way to true achievement!

As an athlete and a coach, I've listened to speakers demand a 110% effort. It's always puzzled me how that was possible. I believed 100% was everything you had.

Mulling over the 110% puzzle over the years I came across an article or book about training that enlightened me. It was a military training manual of some kind. It described 110% as a level of effort that cannot be proven. It exists only as an extraordinarily powerful idea. It can't be quantified and lifts human effort beyond imaginable. To get there, you need imagination, creativity, faith, and belief that there is always a better way. I think about a mom lifting a car to free her trapped young son as one example.

When asked to give 110% I no longer chuckle to myself but go to work with my imagination, creativity, and belief in a better way. And then get there!

PRACTICE OR TRAIN

The basic challenge facing a coach is how to improve the performance of his athletes. This becomes more and more challenging the more talented or skilled the athlete is because the degree of improvement is much smaller and more difficult to achieve. A beginner in any field has so much room for improvement, they will improve with experience without any coaching.

An elite athlete is much closer to his potential. Because elite athletes don't see the great strides in performance a beginner does, they can see their training regimens as tedious, stale, and no longer meaningful in their mind with no immediate results. Without proper coaching, teaching, guidance, and mentoring, top competitors will find themselves plateauing at best, digressing at worst.

The most effective coaches can navigate through this obstacle by selling the athlete on the adage: *It's not the destination, it's the journey that is most rewarding.* In the case of preparing one competitor or a team of competitors, the more joy one finds in the process or journey the more likely they will avoid letdowns in their performance. You may have heard commentators call a team *stale* or *uninspired.*

I often talk to players about practice and training. Practice is defined as habitual action. That is for amateurs. Training is to educate, exercise, refine and discipline specific actions. That is a professional. By understanding the difference, it allows the competitor to think of his daily routine of drills not as tedium but purposeful in refining and disciplining specific actions required to compete and win at the highest level of his trade.

I enjoy watching survival shows on TV. The contestants face some of the toughest, scariest environments on earth and must survive for three weeks. Water, Fire, and Food are essential in survival. Finding water, carrying wood, and starting a fire are tedious but necessary.

No matter what field or career you are pursuing, your training is fundamental to your level of success. I've heard reports of heroic acts where the hero humbly brushes off his actions as just doing his or her job. Most often they will say their training kicked in and they reacted. Professionals train! Amateurs practice!

COACH PLAYERS HARD

I hear head coaches and assistant coaches preach to media, players, and other coaches at clinics that they coach their players hard. I think young professionals have a misguided notion of hard coaching.

To some of the athletes, coaches, media, and aspiring future coaches, this bears the connotation of a hard-driving, profanity-laden, arrogant, mean, and callous approach to coaching. I can't speak for all those who stand up and proclaim that they coach hard, but I'm sure for most of them that is not the impression they would want anyone to have about hard coaching.

How Great Coaches Coach

MY SON-IN-LAW, ERIC - I'M PROUD TO SAY, SERVING OUR COUNTRY FOR THE SECOND TIME

Coaches should spell out exactly what hard coaching entails in the realm of his philosophy and program. Great coaches and leaders spell this out in the process of hiring coaches and recruiting talent. Hard coaching is also misconstrued as "loud coaching". The loudest coach on the field wins the contest for coaching his players the hardest in some programs. Screaming at the top of your lungs from the beginning of the session until the end is not the best way to promote progress and improvement. Raising one's voice can be an effective technique to ensure a critical coaching point hits home. However, when the coach has the volume turned to high at all times, it loses its intent.

- Hard coaching is demanding team members are purpose-driven in all aspects of their work: from the classroom to the field of competition.
- Hard coaching is communicating to the team members what is expected of them and what they can expect from you.
- Hard coaching is demanding that both player and coach follow through with the expectations described.
- Hard coaching is a prescribed process which demands a degree of effort beyond good. Good is not good enough if you want to be the best.

Constant criticism and little praise is also a misconstrued notion of hard coaching as the team members strive for perfection in their performance.

Great coaches can coach hard by praising the model of performance rather than criticizing the undesirable aspect of the team member's performance.

DRILLS OR PLAY FOOTBALL

There are fundamental elements of each position in football that must be mastered in order to reach maximum growth.

These include such things as: stance, start, footwork, change of direction, hand usage, and ball tracking...to name a few.

In the ideal world, these fundamentals should be honed and mastered in the off-season and training camp. Some drills can be done every day in a short period of time for emphasis and muscle memory training. I have heard these commonly referred to as EDDs – the acronym for: "Every Day Drills". Most positions in football can complete their fundamental EDDs in 10 minutes at most.

The rest of the training camp should be centered on group drills, team drills, or offense vs. defense game-like competition. Football is ever-evolving on both sides of the ball and every situation that could occur in a game cannot possibly be drilled. Each player in game-like conditions will experience scenarios they haven't seen before. These valuable competitive repetitions will help them react quickly and correctly on Game Day. It is important that each position group has a block of training time to put players in specific play-related group drills for emphasis. These position-specific group drills can change daily based on opponents or an area of needed improvement.

Educating your team members on situational football is invaluable and must be done with the scripting of a special category of the training regimen. The special categories can include things such as:

- Two Minute
- Short Yardage
- Goal Line
- Third Down
- Fourth Down
- Two-point Conversion
- Last Play

My experience has also made me a firm believer in the idea of playing the game with no script in training sessions as the most valuable of all training repetitions.

Training in this game-like fashion forces players to be able to think and react to an ever-changing landscape of competition. That is the most valuable training one can experience!

How To Coach a Great Player

I am fortunate to have had the opportunity to coach great players. Some of these players may be in the Hall of Fame someday. Some of these players I've worked with were very young in the league with incredible talent, but limited professional experience. Others I have had in their primes, as well as others winding down their career.

A natural thought you have when given the chance to work with a great player who has already had success, is that you must make an impression and gain respect and credibility. Most coaches might think you must teach him something he doesn't know or present a technique or tactic he has never used. That approach can be frustrating not only for the coach, but the player as well.

There will be a time when the player is more receptive to something new than others. When you are starting to develop a healthy coach-player relationship is not the time. Great players have already had success and will resist new ideas and techniques from a new coach they have not yet learned to trust.

A coach or competitor of any kind who wants to improve on the necessary components to grow should study those who are having the greatest success. If you will use that theory, you may someday work with one of those great players you have already studied.

My own philosophy on coaching and teaching a great player is to first learn as much about them as possible well before I would ever start developing a coach-player dialogue. Most importantly, I would study what makes them great -- from competitiveness to techniques, tactics, and scheme.

My initial approach with the players is to learn, coach and reinforce these things the player already does as well as or better than anyone else. A gifted player doesn't even realize what they do because they need no conscious thought to do it. It happens naturally.

By using this method, you are reinforcing the most effective techniques which are producing the best results. In this process, you are also building trust.

As the player's trust grows and his performance continues to improve even if by a small degree, that's when you can comfortably introduce a new technique or approach to attain even greater heights.

How Much Input Do Professional Players Have?

How much input a professional player has depends on how long he has played in the league and how much success he has had. For the most part, the professional level in football is autocratic, not democratic. The coaches develop a game plan and the players carry out the plan.

The degree from which teams will stray from that model depends on a number of things. The confidence level of the head coach and all the coaches around him is the first. If the head coach and his staff are not confident in themselves and their abilities, they will be very hesitant to listen to or give a forum to the players to express their thoughts on how they think the plan versus the upcoming opponent could be more effective. They think allowing input from the player will erode discipline.

Contrary to this thinking, I believe most competitors, when given input into the plan take more ownership. With more ownership, there is more pride in executing the assignments and techniques.

Another factor in how much input players have is related to how much success the team has had. If you are coming off a poor season the coaches are less likely to be open to new ideas from the players.

Proven players who have been successful will have more of an opportunity to express their ideas. A lot depends on the personalities of the players as well. Some players don't want to have any input and actually perform better when they do exactly what they've been coached to do rather than carry the extra burden of ways to improve the plan.

The other side of the coin is the player who performs better when they feel as if they have had a hand in how to attack the opponent most effectively. From my experience, I have found by involving the players who want to contribute not only helps the player, but the coach as well.

I have also found adjustments that must be made quickly on game day are more readily received and executed when the player is invested. When coaches are very rigid during preparation, players are more reluctant to buy in.

Know your personnel! Involve those who want to be involved. Communicate the plays or techniques that have no room for discussion and why.

How Do Teams Cope with Injuries?

Injuries are inevitable in the game of football. Management, coaches, and players all realize adjustments will have to be made during the course of a season because of missed time by players due to injury. There is some luck involved in winning a championship relative to injuries. Regardless of how well you prepare, there are injuries that all the planning in the world probably will not prevent.

The injuries you hope to limit, but will never completely prevent, are overuse injuries. These are injuries that can be reduced by education of safe technique, conditioning, hydrating, and heat and cold environments. Proper diagnosis by the training and medical staff is important to how much time it will take for the athlete to return to the field. Many times, the players themselves want to return to the playing field so badly they return too quickly and worsen the injury.

Because injuries are going to happen, acquiring not only first level talent, but depth on your team is critical to sustainable success. That is a balancing act of resources (mainly salary cap implications) to roster top notch starters, but adequate backups.

The standard coaching mantra when a player is injured is: *next man up!* This means the backup steps in and you move on without skipping a beat. Confidence is fragile and can be shaken if leadership doesn't approach injuries with the *next man up* attitude. If the coaches panic or show a lack of confidence -- so will the players. The reality of injuries is that most often the injured player's replacement is not as talented and productive or he would be starting. At times, a team will have a rash of injuries that make it almost impossible to sustain winning. Injuries to a starting quarterback are especially devastating. It is difficult enough to find one quarterback, let alone two.

How is it then that some teams overcome injuries to key players?

The first thing that occurs is that the coaching staff does a tremendous job of adjusting the scheme as necessary to emphasize a different aspect of their team to maximize their production. Next, the remaining starters increase their level of performance. At times, this happens because they simply get more opportunity to produce due to the injury. If a wide receiver gets injured and he was the number one receiver, then the number two ranked receiver may get more passes thrown his way and becomes a star. The same can occur on the defensive side of the ball.

Great teams overcome adversity because they have good coaching staffs that can adapt and have depth to navigate the bumps in the road. Make no mistake, when the best players are injured the team is simply not as good, but great organizations find a way to win!

THE NFL INTERVIEW PROCESS

Each organization conducts interviews a little differently. Every head coach has his own way to interview candidates as well. I've been present for well over a dozen coaching interviews. Most often the first thing done is to introduce yourself and your existing staff to the candidate. Make them feel at home and comfortable. Use this part of the process as an opportunity to sell your first-class organization.

After introductions, when you are short on experience and young in the profession, there is normally a segment of the process to gauge your knowledge and expertise in the subject matter required for your position. In the coaching world, this is called "being put on the board".

Being put on the board used to mean going to the chalkboard and detailing your X and O knowledge as well as answering any questions with which you are bombarded. It can be an intimidating process for a young candidate. It is important for both the employer and candidate because the employer determines if the candidate has the expertise necessary while the candidate gains confidence in presenting his material under stress.

Even when the candidate is not selected, the experience of the interview and being on the board is invaluable for the future. I had coached fifteen years before I was experienced enough and had a resume to prove it before I was interviewed and not put on the board.

Regardless of a candidate's experience and reputation, it is wise to have them present a list of the subject matter and systems they have coached in. These sessions don't have to be as detailed as with an inexperienced candidate. You will be surprised how eager even a seasoned coach is to display his knowledge! Never assume a candidate has the expertise you feel would qualify him for your team. Once they are on your team it is too late. All other aspects of the expertise segment concern who the candidate on the board should be presenting to.

I have experienced everything from interviews with just the head coach to the whole staff or a mixture. I believe the interview should be conducted by the head coach and the candidate's immediate supervisor who is the coordinator. I feel candidates can feel a little insulted when they must present to peers or coworkers, not superiors during these sessions. It can also appear to the candidate as an intelligence gathering opportunity more than an interview. Candidates will share more information with superiors than with peers.

After the introduction and subject matter phase, some organizations will tour the facility, have lunch or dinner, and send the candidate on his way. One of the best and most thorough interviews I had was when I was sent to spend time with each member of the staff in a low-key fashion so they could get a feel for my personality and to see if it would mesh with the staff as a whole. Then there was the exit meeting with the coordinator and head coach.

Talent acquisition is the most important aspect of building a champion. Leave no stone unturned and be sure to check with previous employers when possible, for feedback.

No matter how great strategies and tactics are, it is mainly impossible to sustain success without talent!

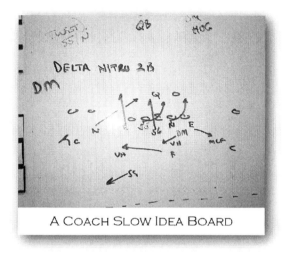

A COACH SLOW IDEA BOARD

THE INTERVIEW: A PUBLIC RELATIONS AND MARKETING TOOL

The interview process is a critical element in locating and acquiring the necessary talent to build a championship team. There is a secondary aspect of the interview process that organizations and leaders sometimes overlook. Not only are you interviewing the candidate and potential team member, they are conducting their own interview.

Whether the interview candidates are offered the position or not, they are forming an opinion of you as a leader, your organization, your staff, your commitment to winning, as well as your facilities. Many organizations and leaders have fumbled the ball in this area.

Not only should you be looking for the best fit for your organization to help pave the way to a championship, but you are conducting a public relations campaign and marketing strategy to promote your team and orga-

THE BEST DAUGHTERS-IN-LAW YOU COULD HAVE,
LUCY AND VAL.

nization. Leave all candidates with the feeling they would be honored to be part of your organization. Those candidates you did not choose (if they were treated correctly) will look for a future opportunity to fit on your team and will tell other peers what a committed, first-class organization you are — one destined for success.

So many leaders have candidates exit the process with a feeling of your arrogance, callousness, and overall sterile environment. This day and age has lost the simplest class act of at least informing all candidates of their decision. The norm is the only person who receives communication is the candidate who is hired.

As you conduct your interview in a first class, upbeat manner you are also doing the best job possible to ensure the candidate you wish to bring aboard will accept the position and be excited to do so.

Think of the interview process as not only acquiring top talent, but a promotional opportunity for the organization to help you acquire future talent!

INVISIBLE PROGRESS

Often the bottom line -- or in the coaching world, wins and losses -- don't tell the whole story. Coaching staff changes are

OUR GRANDSON, TYE
- PROGRESS IN ACTION

made by head coaches and in increasingly faster fashion. When results aren't immediately evident someone is going to pay the price.

As these changes are becoming more and more common, it is very easy for these quickdraw changes to become the norm. The norm doesn't make it right. It also makes future leaders and head coaches more callous and even cavalier in executing the staff changes. At times the changes do provide a spark to a team and lead to some short-lived success. Owners are also becoming less patient with head coaches.

The new age of technology and video games can create an unrealistic mentality. Players can be thought of like a video game player controlled by the computer's artificial intelligence. Players in real life cannot be operated by someone else's intelligence and ability. Once the human element is removed from the decision-making it is too easy to place blame and make changes without fully contemplating the consequences to those affected by the decision.

There have been few if any instances I can remember of the leaders who made a change that didn't provide desired results, to be held accountable in any way. Most often they were applauded for making tough decisions. When ample time is given with no progress, there are times change is necessary. Ample time can be debated and is ultimately decided by leadership.

I'd like to relate a story that may provide food for thought for head coaches, future head coaches, and leaders.

OUR GRANDDAUGHTER, AVERIE - PROGRESS IN ACTION

A dad and his three sons made a trip to the batting cages to get ready for the upcoming baseball season. The two older boys (ages eight and fifteen) took turns with the machine making consistently good contact. They were both excited and confident for practice to begin.

The youngest son took his turn. With fifteen pitches per token, he took fifteen pitches and fifteen whiffs. The seven-year-old did not even come close. As you would expect of a seven-year-old who watched his brothers hit every pitch, the tears flowed. "Let me try again," was his next response. Another token and another fifteen whiffs. More tears, more whiffs, and more tokens. After four rounds the dad was almost in tears much like the seven-year-old suffering through each whiff. The dad almost couldn't bear the suffering of watching the boy fail again and again. One more round and again all whiffs. Not even a foul ball. Zero contact. The youngest screamed, "The ball is invisible!"

The next evening the two oldest boys wanted another trip to the batting cages and the youngest reluctantly went along. After watching his brothers for a few rounds he decided to give it another try. "Oh no" the dad thought. Here goes another tear-filled night of swinging at the invisible pitches. In the cage he goes, readies himself and the bat, here comes the first pitch and 'BAM' contact. A well struck line drive right up the middle. Then fourteen more pitches and not one single whiff. High fives all around. What joy on his face!

I should know, I was there because it was me and my three sons. The lesson I learned was that although I didn't see progress with whiff after whiff, progress was being made. Slowly his eyes were being trained. His timing was getting better even though there were no visible signs. His determination and persistence were getting stronger through the tears. Then all of a sudden, results became evident.

Sometimes the bottom line doesn't tell the whole story. Progress is being made even though it is not seen. "A man scatters seed on the ground; he sleeps and rises-night and day, and the seed sprouts and grows-he doesn't know how." (Mark 4:26-27)

ENJOY THE GRIND

So much of today's world is centered around the end result. It is the bottom line and wins and losses in the world of coaching.

With players, it's about statistics regarding touchdowns, passer rating, tackles, sacks, batting average, three point shots, monthly sales, new memberships, and the list goes on and on.

The social media world has worked its way into every profession including sports.

Coaches and players not only consume themselves with the bottom line but have drifted away from the team aspect into the world of branding. Some coaches and players are trying to draw attention to themselves rather than the common goal of the team.

It is important to prepare yourself for the future but not at the expense of team goals, values, and rules. The new rage in coaching lingo is the word "process". Process is a series of actions or steps taken to achieve a particular end.

In any profession, the process will differ from team to team and organization to organization. The head coach or leader of an organization will have a process they have developed that they believe will lead them to the goal or objective. In the NFL, the head coach has a vision of the process by which his team will win the Super Bowl.

The most successful coaches can sell the team members on the concept that in order to achieve greatness they must forget greatness.

Instead of the focus being on the end result, it is most important to focus on the process itself. The day-to-day actions that will take the team closer to the objective one step at a time. I hear coaches talking with the media and saying how their team is starting to understand the process. In most cases the steps needed to attain a high level of achievement are very difficult.

Therefore, it is easy to lose focus, become fatigued physically and mentally, and lose motivation to continue the process toward achievement. That is why most achievements come after the grind of a difficult process necessary to attain the goal.

When leaders can inspire their team members to enjoy and embrace the grind (hard, dull, work) they are on their way to achieving greatness.

Greatness is not achieved by striving to be great, but by being great grinding towards your goal. Enjoy the grind and you never know what you will find.

EMBRACE THE GAME

Somewhere, the idea of competitive sports has received the label of being a bad thing; especially for our youth. That attitude also filters into other areas of our society. Philosophically, we have moved from the field of competition to participation awards. I've watched my children as often as I could, work their way through the old world competitive youth sports programs. I've seen them go through good teams, poor teams, great coaches, good coaches, and not so good coaches.

I will say all the coaches of youth sports should be commended for sacrificing their time to work with our kids. Every coach I'm sure has the intentions of helping our children find success and enjoy the field of competition. I think that is where we lose track. The real world is competitive. Even in the most ideal of circumstances the world will be globally competitive.

ME WITH RYAN'S FAMILY
(L TO R: TYE, ME, RYAN, VALERIE, AND AVERIE)

Rather than shelter our youth from the competitive aspect of society we should teach our young ones to embrace it.

I was an NFL coach for over twenty years and I am ecstatic to see the coaching world with the likes of Pete Carroll who coaches in an enthusiastic, positive, energetic fashion that teaches men to embrace competition. His athletes learn to enjoy competition and the challenges set before them. It is the competition itself that becomes the attraction. Winning or losing is the measuring stick of competition.

Enjoy winning because it is difficult to do if you are striving to become the best. If it is not enjoyable to win then there is no longer the passion to win. When the team wins, it's important everybody wins. That is the goal. When we lose, everybody has a hand in the loss. When you don't win, it is important to treat that setback as a lesson. Learn from the experience and correct the things you can and look forward to the next challenge.

Finally, wins and losses decide the competition. Wins and losses do not define us. Doing the best with what we have been given is what will define our character.

Let us also be reminded that competition does exist within the team. It is important that team members understand the team always comes first. Decisions made are for the best interests of the team. When the team wins all win. Each team member contributes his or her share to the common goal.

Talent, experience, and opportunity are some reasons the amount of each one's contribution to the team may differ. Each team member is important to reaching the goal. There are times based on the overall strategy to accomplish the goal that one team member's area of expertise may be highlighted over others.

Being a member of a team means respecting the chain of command and putting the team's goals ahead of any individual goals. Leaders understand how to develop a competitive edge by maintaining a team mentality in the world of wins and losses. Have a passion for good and do good with a passion.

My Take

PASSION GENERATES
THE HEAT TO BURN
THROUGH THE MOST
DIFFICULT OBSTACLES.

COACH SLOW

I guess like anyone lucky enough to have been associated with the NFL, I get asked questions all the time about what it's really like.

Not only do I thoroughly enjoy conversations with these knowledgeable and enthusiastic fans, I enjoy the opportunity to personally reflect on the successes and challenges I had the privilege of experiencing.

Like every sports lover, I relish offering my distinctive opinions about the good, the bad, and the ugly about the greatest game in the world.

SIDELINE EXPERIENCE

A professional football game, much like any event that is broad-cast on TV, is so much different when seen in person. That is especially true the closer you get to the action. A football game seen from the sideline is much different than being at the stadium watching from the top row. The farther you get from the field and higher you go, the more you can see the big picture and the whole field.

Coaches and knowledgeable fans who enjoy the tactics of the game plan may prefer that view because you can see the play unfold before your eyes on offense and defense. From that vantage point you get a video game type of viewpoint. You don't hear the sounds of the game, nor is the speed of the game as evident.

RYAN AND ANDREA ENJOYING THE PRE-GAME

The general's view of the battlefield is far different than that of the foot soldier in the battle. On or near the sideline restricts your view of the whole field. You can only see one side if you are close to the ball. You can see more of the field if you have the freedom to move farther back from the offense or defense. The sounds of the game are fascinating. Players making calls to one another not only verbally, but with hand signals in what would seem a foreign language to most fans. Hand signals that are so subtle, but can describe a whole play for the players on the field.

The size and speed of the athletes is much more noticeable on the sidelines when you see players next to the average person. When they are on the field together it is not as noticeable since most are similar in size relative to their position. The speed of the game is amazing and frightening at times even for a veteran of the sideline. There are some violent collisions and the sound of those collisions is a heavy thud of bodies, pads, and helmets!

There is little communication during the play, just the noise of shoes on turf or grass and the sight of turf being kicked up or the rubber granules of field turf letting loose. Most players are focused on their job and don't want or need the distraction.

When you are on the sideline you must be aware at all times. Many players make their way to the sideline and if you are not attentive to the action or don't have the ability to quickly get out of the way you can easily be hurt. Although the sideline's view is restricted, there is nowhere else you can appreciate the real game!!

GAME DAY ADJUSTMENTS

It is a common belief that many adjustments to a game occur at halftime. In professional football the halftime limit is twelve minutes unless otherwise specified. That twelve-minute limit starts at the end of the second quarter. It is awfully short. Players need time to attend to themselves for various things such as taping, re-taping, equipment, hydration, and just a minute or two to settle down and mentally unwind.

Position coaches need time to review specifics and coordinators need time to make adjustments and give players an assessment of the first half performance. The head coach will need a minute to address the full team.

When I was a coordinator I believed all of the segments were important. As a defensive coordinator, I would allocate four minutes to the players, four minutes to the coordinator and three minutes to the position coaches. This allowed the head coach one minute to make his points. Obviously, the head coach would take as much time as he wanted so the position coaches' time was fluid. Four minutes to make more than one or two major changes in a game plan is not nearly enough time.

It is important to remember that the game evolves in real time on the field. Between offensive and defensive series coaches can get a lot accomplished especially if the other side of the ball is on the field for an extended amount of time. The really good coaches make changes throughout the game and don't wait until halftime.

Play callers must recognize whether their plan needs immediate adjustments. They must identify and respond to their opponent as quickly as possible. They must be patient enough to allow the plan to unfold. They also can't be afraid to change the plan when it is evident it is not working. When a coordinator abandons a plan too quickly or is too stubborn to change a plan, it will affect the players' confidence and mentality. It is a slippery slope and great coaches navigate it well. If a play caller doesn't manage the flow of the game as the season wears on, their players can lose confidence in the coach. At times the best adjustment is no adjustment. At other times, some teams and players make phenomenal adjustments.

Peyton Manning was a master of adjusting plans at halftime. I believe you need a first half plan and have a second half with some new wrinkles. Great coaches feel the game and see the plan quickly.

TODAY'S COACHING AND TEACHING CHALLENGE

Coaching and teaching in today's environment can present a very real challenge. I've always believed coaching is teaching. I was fortunate to be trained by coaches who felt the same. Organization was paramount to preparing your lesson plan or practice plan for each day. Every minute was mapped out in detail. Every drill, technique, and play was presented in a logical progression. The meetings with players were prepared just as diligently.

Today's challenge for educators and in some cases coaches, is the gradual rise in the attitude that students don't fail -- teachers fail the students.

I'm sure in any profession there are those who do not put the effort, planning, and passion into their work and ultimately do fail their students or players. More often than not, in today's world of participation trophies, it is used merely as an excuse for the student or player.

The teacher-student or coach-player relationship is a two-way street. Both parties must put forth their best effort to succeed.

One of my favorite quotes regarding coaching is: "I can teach you, but I can't learn you."

A coach or teacher can present material in an exciting, creative, and easy-to-understand way but cannot learn for the student or player.

Dedicated coaches and players put in one-on-one time for students seeking assistance for concepts they may not grasp readily. It is proven that the best method to learn is to see it, hear it, write it, and speak it regarding subject material; and then you can own it.

As a coach, I've always taken great pride watching my players or unit improve and produce to the best of their ability. In my teaching, I also took pride in my players' ability and desire to learn. I took it as a challenge if a player needed extra tutoring. People learn in different ways. Often a player needed the material presented in a different fashion or needed the subject matter communicated a little differently than in the group environment.

When leadership is honest and objective in evaluating coaches or teachers they will acknowledge that there are times when a player or student has reached his competency level.

Not that a player or student won't be able to learn, but may not be able to learn at the pace or speed necessary to produce at that level of their profession.

In my NFL experience, it was often stated that mental errors by players were on the coaches. When head coaches hire great teachers, it should also be understood there may be some players who just can't pick up the material for the speed, volume, and stress necessary for useful application on the battlefield. There are rare times a player is so talented the leader may be willing to adjust his game plan because of that limitation.

It is very difficult to justify an adjustment in a philosophy or playbook for one player.

If there are more players or students who can't seem to grasp the playbook, then it should be considered the playbook is too complicated for the speed of the game.

If it is only one position that has many challenges, then the coach or leader should be considered as one of the possible reasons.

Leadership should make all of those assessments privately. There have been organizations where the players were told that mental errors were coaching. I wasn't a fan of that presentation technique because it gave any player or student an immediate excuse to blame others.

Great coaches, teachers, and leaders inspire their team to work with coaches to learn the game plan.

Do The Best Players Always Play?

The best players always play, eventually. Sometimes there may be a player on the sideline who is a better player at the moment than the player who is a starter and on the field. This can be the case for a number of reasons. The most common reason is that a team or organization signs a free agent for big money or drafts a player very high in the first round and has a large financial commitment. That organization, because of its financial commitment, is going to give the player every opportunity to earn that money invested in him, even if in the short term there may be a player watching from the sideline who would perform better.

When organizations do this, they are assuming the more talented player will catch up and easily surpass the player he is replacing. In most instances that is the case, but not always and that is why you hear the term "bust" being thrown around. When the financial commitment or draft status of a player doesn't match his performance level is when you have a bust.

The general manager or head coach is usually the person deciding how much time you give a player to prove himself before you move on and put the best player on the field. Depending on the organization's chain of command, there can sometimes be a difference of opinion on who is the best player. When there is a general manager in charge of personnel and the head coach in charge of football, there can be times they are not in complete agreement. Evaluation is subjective. It is therefore natural there will be differences of opinion.

Much like the previous scenario, the real decision is how much patience do you have to wait for the player to produce? If there is internal friction within an organization it is mostly because there is a difference of opinion about a number of items. Individual talent and where to focus your resources in acquiring the talent to build the team are the biggest points of contention.

There have been occasions in my experience where anyone who was drafted from rounds one through three was automatically a starter and the fourth rounder you could count on as making the team.

Coaches like the players who give them the best chances to win immediately and who make few mental errors. At times, the personnel department likes the new talent or the players who give the best chance to win in the future. There will always be some differences of opinion, but the people who can work through them with open and honest communication to get the best players on the field will find the most success.

BRANDING

Over my twenty years in the NFL, a lot has changed. Free Agency was originated my second year in the league while I was coaching for the Chicago Bears. There have been between twenty or thirty rule changes. Most of the rule changes have benefited the offense. Offenses have become pass-oriented and defenses have become more versatile and sophisticated. Defense has become more specialized as well.

Many teams have built new stadiums to make the venue more fan-friendly. Reality shows have found popularity. Players' and coaches' salaries have improved dramatically. Games can be accessed now almost anywhere with a mobile device.

Today, players are better trained and are very proficient in this age of social media. Players are much more informed about health risks and the fact their professional football career will last only a short time and there's a small window of opportunity for top earning power.

Most players now have to consider what they will do when the window of opportunity closes. They must prepare for a career after playing. Coaches must be prepared to find a new line of work as well since patience to win is a novelty. The popularity of sports on television or on your iPad or computer has never been higher. There are pre-game shows, post-game shows, and everything in-between.

All of these things contribute to players and coaches trying to promote their own brand. Football is a team game and no one is bigger than the game. Some players and coaches see the game as a way to promote themselves and their own brand. That is one of the reasons you see so much celebration or anything that will bring media attention to themselves. To these players, positive or negative on-field attention is better than getting no attention at all. This is also the case with some coaches.

This mentality by players and coaches chips away the foundation of the game; namely Team. These competitors don't see themselves as someone who's the face of a team, but as an entertainer using the team to grow his brand. This mentality is a selfish mindset and ultimately not good for the team or the game if this attitude grows.

Some of the other approaches to the game can be businessman, warrior, student, or discipline.

The businessman approach is a very serious one. In it, the player and coach know it is their job and approach everything in that fashion. These are the players and coaches who chose the paycheck and are not interested in anything that won't help pad their paycheck. This is a growing mentality with free agency.

There are many warriors in the league. These players love and crave the competition. They enjoy being part of a team, especially in a leadership role and will not stand for a teammate not giving his all. They display enthusiasm, vigor, courage, and aggressiveness.

Another personality is the martial artist. One who sees football as a discipline or in other words, a way of life. This player not only prepares in the office, but outside as well. Every area of his life is part of that discipline including extra strength and conditioning, nutrition, sleep, studying and anything that will help the team win. Regardless of the approach taken, the great players also take a student's approach. Assuming nothing, constantly learning, and applying a beginner's mind.

Branding is part of the business and is important for the time when the door closes for players and coaches. The vast majority of the players and coaches place it second to the priority of their team and the game.

There are so many warriors, students, and unselfish competitors it is disrespectful to them when a player's only objective is to call attention to themselves.

Play Calling Palate

When dining at a restaurant you are given a menu of items to choose from. Each person will receive the same menu. The number of items on the menu will vary depending on the restaurant's philosophy. Do they specialize in seafood, steaks, hamburgers, chicken, or pasta? Some restaurants will try to serve many different items. Once the customer is ready they place an order from the menu.

If you had a dinner party of eight, even though everyone had the same menu there will be eight different orders based on each individual taste.

Play calling is very similar to ordering from a menu. If all play callers had the same call sheet or menu, the game would still take on many different complexions depending on the personality, philosophy, and the taste of each individual play caller. Some play callers are aggressive while others are conservative.

There are instances when you hear of the head coach taking over the play calling or relinquishing that duty. If you wonder if that can make a difference even though the plays or the players may not have changed, the answer is "Yes!" Like any task or skill, everyone has a slightly different level of expertise, competency, and execution.

Many factors are involved. Performance under pressure plays a big part. Does the play caller go through the emotional highs and lows of the game and let it affect their objectivity in decision making? Do they stick with the plan developed during the week when you have the most objective view of what is best for the game week opponent, or do they abandon quickly? The opposite scenario can also be true if the play caller is too stubborn or committed to a plan that clearly isn't working.

A play caller must be like the Kenny Rogers song "know when to hold 'em and know when to fold 'em". You never know what kind of caller you will get until that person actually calls the game. One game is not enough data to know what you have. It will take at least a full season to get the experience needed to truly evaluate a play caller's talent and personality.

One of the other influential factors affecting a play caller can be the talent or strength and weakness of his own team or the opponent. Obviously, a great play caller takes advantage of his strength and exposes the weakness of the opponent. Some play callers are influenced by fear. Fear of giving up a big play. A lack of confidence in your players' execution can keep a coordinator from making a call that wasn't properly executed during the week.

Play callers can be influenced too much by the head coach when his calls are constantly criticized post-game. The play caller then makes decisions based on the way he thinks the head coach would. A play caller being anyone but himself simply doesn't work.

Play callers can also be influenced by players. A player or players may complain or ask for certain plays that highlight them. At times the suggestions are constructive and other times don't fit the big picture, but will be used for fear of offending the player. The play caller must be confident in himself and his plan, commit to it and let the chips fall where they may!

WHY SOME HEAD COACHES CALL PLAYS

Most NFL head coaches do not call plays. That duty is delegated to the offensive and defensive coordinators. The head coach is able to have a much better grasp of the game management scenarios when he is not a play caller. He can be much more aware of decisions to be made regarding penalties, field goals or punts, going for the first down on fourth down, timeout utilization, two minute tactics, and a much better awareness of the overall effectiveness of both the offense and defense and special teams.

Most head coaches are promoted to a head coaching position after spending years as an offensive or defensive coordinator. They were most certainly play callers in their coordinator's role. They likely had great success which catapulted them into the position of head coach.

Game Day is the most exciting, exhilarating, rewarding, and fun part of coaching. This is especially true if you are the play caller. It is a human chess match between you and the opposing play caller.

You as the play caller has the most influence on the game's outcome next to the players on the field themselves. That is what makes the game so stressful and thrilling at the same time. It is also the reason some head coaches continue to call plays. Why do some head coaches call plays? Because it's thrilling and FUN!

PASSION OR FURY

Emotions run high in the game of football. It is a game where one team is pitted against another in a battle of real estate. It is not only a contact sport but a game of collision.

Once you step on the field there is no place to hide. It is a game of superiority. Each team striving to display dominance over the other.

Once you cross the line and onto the field of competition you must be all in. You cannot play well unless you are completely committed. There's only one speed and that is full speed. Playing any less than full speed is dangerous to yourself and your teammates.

The Most Successful on the Football Field are Passionate About the Game

Passion is defined as an intense desire or enthusiasm for something, a strong and barely controllable emotion. Passion and enthusiasm for a good cause are beneficial to achieving your goal and reaching your destination. Football also requires a tremendous amount of focus to diagnose fast-moving parts and instantly react to fit properly into the scheme and strategy of the play called.

Because of the physical and violent nature of the game, it's important to be disciplined mentally, physically, and emotionally.

When Adversity Strikes or Your Opponent is Getting the Better of You, it is Important Passion Doesn't Turn into Fury

Fury is defined as an intense rage, wild and violent anger. Passion is a barely controllable emotion and without discipline can switch in an instant to fury. Fury does not belong in the game. Any player not able to control his passion will hinder his performance and the team's.

All coaches love players who are passionate about the game. Players who go from passion to fury on the field will become a distraction and ultimately cost their team games. Passion is a necessity to play such a demanding game. "It is better to be fiery hot or icy cold because if you are lukewarm I will spit you out." (Revelation 3:15)

NFL Off-Season Limitations

The Collective Bargaining Agreement between the NFL and the NFLPA (players' union) has had some positive impacts.

On the other hand, some of the rules have had some negative results as well. Once a team ends its season there is a no contact period with players until the third week of April or the first week of April if your team has hired a new coach.

For some players, that will mean three months of no contact. This non-contact rule, which includes any form of communication, was the players' idea. At the time, it seemed like an idea that had sound reasoning.

As with many things, you can gain a better perspective over time.

NFLPA Non-Contact Period - Impact on Veteran Players

Not considered detrimental to the seasoned veteran who has solidified his roster spot and role on the team. These are the players who form the nucleus of the team. (We are talking about six to ten players on each team. They have reached a high level of success and established themselves as the team's stars.) In their case, three months to take needed time off to heal and re-energize is important.

CAROL AT THE GREENBRIAR HOTEL IN WEST VIRGINIA, ENJOYING A BREAK AFTER A LONG SEASON

It is also beneficial because most of these players have the finances to hire a personal trainer who knows the specific needs of the player. It can be strength, flexibility, and conditioning in nature or relate to his specific positional techniques. This is a positive outcome of the rule.

Impact on Rookies

The players who are not established as proven players are being hindered in their desire to improve their skill set. This is a three-month period they could voluntarily work with their coaches on understanding, processing, and digesting the playbook. It is a time also to view video to grow in understanding concepts and opponents' tendencies.

They could work with coaches on exercising, educating, and refining specific actions necessary for their position.

To help all the players who want to spend time at the facility improving, it might be a good idea to compromise and allow anyone with four years or less of accrued seasons, the opportunity to train with their team.

This would benefit the majority of the players, not just the few.

THE NFL DRAFT: EVALUATION TECHNIQUES

In professional football, acquiring players through the NFL Draft or signing a player through free agency are the two dominant ways of acquiring talent for your team.

My journey in professional football allowed me to experience various evaluation techniques and philosophies. The first thing the organization must determine: Is your team relatively close to championship level talent or do you have a long way to go?

This determination cannot be done lightly. Quality or quantity is the question. If it is determined your team is close, that could dictate a path of acquiring only a few game-changing or high-quality acquisitions that could bring your team to a championship level.

ME AFTER A WORKOUT WITH TWO NFL DRAFT PROSPECTS

This is sometimes a very risky path because those types of players require a high-dollar and high-profile commitment. When their production matches the financial commitment, it is a positive experience for the team and organization.

Then there are a couple of negative ramifications if these high-dollar and high-profile commitment players do not perform at an elite level. The first is the simple fact that the expectation level of your team is the championship and anything less means your commitment to those few players was a failure.

The other negative could impact the chemistry of the locker room. When a newly acquired player is signed as one of the highest paid players on your team, if they do not produce to match their pay it creates friction in the locker room. If the evaluation of your own talent points to many weaknesses, the philosophy to acquire talent would lean to quantity; requiring as many draft picks as possible and possibly unloading high-priced team members as you build for the near future.

Regardless of the quality or quantity path, there is an evaluation process that takes place to identify the players or candidates your organization will target. The initial stages of evaluating talent is similar in all organizations:

- The personnel department and its team of scouts evaluate draft-eligible players in their area and give them a grade.
- The position coaches are given a list by the personnel department of players who are draft-worthy of their position and they will give those players a grade. This first level process is common.

It is from here I've seen the techniques branch off in many directions.

The one technique that proved extremely effective was having the personnel grade, rate, and list each player by position.

So the quarterbacks for example were graded and then listed from best to worst. Each position was ranked in that manner, the grades were determined by watching game video of each player. A minimum of four games was necessary to assign a grade.

The more game video or data, the closer you were to gaining a clear picture of the player's talent. Once the coaches finished their grading and ranking each position, the coach would be called to meet with the general manager, head coach, and scouting department.

The coach would present his ranking and a brief description of the player's strengths and weaknesses. When the coach finished his presentation, the personnel department's rankings were revealed.

Any major discrepancies would then be evaluated in a case by case fashion. This was done by watching the player's best games together and then the GM would adjust the ranking if he felt it was necessary. The personnel department's ranking served as the baseline.

The Process of Elimination

This particular system also had a unique way of eliminating some players:

- Through thorough discussions with the coaches on the most important characteristics of their position based on height, weight, and speed were determined.
- Any player not satisfying that minimum and maximum parameter would not make the draft board.

- From my standpoint, this was the best and most successful of all the systems I experienced.
- The minimum and maximum parameter does not imply that all players who didn't fit that category couldn't make a team.

The GM believed that anyone not fitting the parameters should be tried out by another team and let them assume the risk. If the player proves himself on another team, they could still be acquired by free agency at some point.

I chose this format because it proved to be the most effective in the percentage of hits on talent.

Offensive Play Calling Mentality

I've been a defensive coach my whole career and am a bit jealous of the offense for several reasons.

The first is how the rules and rule changes are designed for basically two reasons as the game of professional football evolves.

The number one reason is for the safety of the players.

Another reason is to ensure the scoring average of the game either increases or maintains because most fans enjoy a higher scoring game than a defensive masterpiece. This of course gives the offense the advantage.

The second reason is that the offense dictates the defense by what personnel they decide to put on the field. Defensive tactics usually, but not always, react to what the offense puts on the field. The offensive play caller can go from play to play as quickly and effectively as he wishes and dictate the action.

An offensive coordinator who calls plays may have a game day call sheet of 100 plays. If it wasn't for down and distance and field position, he could close his eyes and point to his chart and make a call. There is a tremendous amount of time and study that goes into the call list. It is based on what is anticipated of the defense by endlessly studying video of the opponent.

My main point is the offense is proactive in nature and the defense reactive in nature.

That is why I, as a defensive play caller, always liked an aggressive, pressure-oriented scheme because I always felt it could give the defense the feeling they were the one dictating the action.

COACHES DON'T HAVE HOBBIES

The coaching profession is a demanding, stressful, grueling grind of long hours, sometimes tedious work, and little free time. Professional coaches work seven days a week, about sixteen hours a day from August until February. Because it requires such a commitment, most coaches are extremely passionate about their work and really love what they do.

In my case, I loved the teaching aspect in the classroom and on the field. It was such a pleasure to see the players improve and have success. I also have a curious side and with all the resources available to study tactics and strategy, I loved when I had a chance to use the creative part of my brain.

When the season ends and after a short vacation, the off-season doesn't offer much more of a break. Expect to make it home for dinner and have some free weekends, but as the pressure of winning increases so do the hours. Professional coaches are paid very well and much is expected of them. Arriving at the office before 5:30am year-round is not out of the ordinary.

Head coaches expect nothing but an obsession with your job and nothing but tunnel vision and razor-sharp focus on football and every aspect of it. There are no sick days, doctors' appointments, picking your kids up from school, meeting your wife for lunch, or even admission of a hobby outside of coaching football.

Passion for the game and your job is necessary, but all of us need to coach the brain in areas other than Xs and Os at times to stay mentally and emotionally healthy. Most coaches are very bright and need to stimulate the intellect so they don't get stale.

A hobby is not a bad thing even if it is a quick workout or thirty minutes of switching gears to read an article on something other than football. We just don't want to admit it for fear we be accused of lacking the commitment.

The Holidays for Coaches

The holiday season from Thanksgiving through the New Year can be a wonderful time with the family. Christmas for young children is magical and such a joy to watch. It is also a great time of year to renew our faith and be thankful for our blessings.

For those whose chosen career is coaching football, the holiday season is much different. The stress can dampen the holiday spirit. Some coaches are getting ready for a big game and others are worried about keeping their jobs. Coaches working for teams that didn't meet expectations or coaches whose individual unit did not reach the expectation level of the head coach are worried about the next paycheck.

VAL, RYAN, TYE, AND AVERIE
— BEING HAPPY AND STRONG FOR THE HOLIDAYS

Whether you are a young coaching family or a veteran coaching family it takes a toll. I remember all too well my younger coaching days when my future paycheck was in question. Both my wife and I would do our best to keep our spirits up around our four young children. No matter how hard we tried there were times the stress would break through the hard exterior we had built. My faith and the support of my wife and family is what helped me through the dark times.

> "...Darkness covers the earth and total darkness the peoples; but the Lord will shine over you." (Isaiah 60:2)

The head coach being let go is what the media emphasizes. The head coach is the celebrity and most recognizable by the public so the media attention is expected. The assistant coaches are rarely mentioned but most affected. They don't have the financial security of most head coaches and will have a much more difficult time finding a new employer. Assistant coach changes are simply a news flash at best on the ticker tape. The coaching world is not for anyone seeking job security. The holiday season or should I say the "firing season" is not a time relished by many football coaches.

I have always been inspired when I hear athletes going through a rough patch maintaining their optimism and persistence proclaiming that God has a plan. I applaud such belief, but worry some people may think that their future is predetermined by God's plan. God is all knowing. All knowing is not all causing. We will be defined by our own choices. Being strong in faith will give us confidence in our choices. By faith we know God will not forsake us.

I love the footprints in the sand poem:

"...But I have noticed that during the most trying periods of my life there have been only one set of footprints in the sand. Why, when I needed you most you have not been there for me?"

The Lord replied, "The times when you have seen only one set of footprints is when I carried you." [6]

There will be many changes every year. Some will be well publicized head coaching changes and other assistant coach changes. Some changes are necessary. Some changes are not necessary but rationalized by the decision makers to be the best for the organization.

Only the one deciding the fates of the coaches actually knows which of the two it is. Often the fans and media applaud the firing. The heads must roll approach keeps criticism at bay for a short time.

After enjoying the holiday season and welcoming in the new year, please keep the coaches in your prayers as they battle through the difficult time of the firing and hiring season.

ANNUAL "SANTA BOWL" - CHRISTMAS DAY FOOTBALL
WITH MY SONS AND GRANDSON
(L TO R: STEVE, ME, TYE, RYAN AND BOBBY)

HILLS AND HEART, HEART AND HILLS

Conditioning is a major part of all sports. Vince Lombardi said: "Fatigue makes cowards of us all."

Training your body and mind for the competition you will face is the best way to combat fatigue. In the sports world, this requires a tremendous amount of physical training. Strength training for the muscles, cardiovascular training for the heart and lungs -- those combine to train our mental toughness.

Every sport has a specific type of physical conditioning.

Football is a series of short all-out bursts of activity followed by a short rest interval and repeated over a three to four-hour period of time. It requires speed and power combined with grace and a strength of will pitting one man vs. another or one team vs. another.

Basketball on the other hand is a contest of constant action that bounces between sprints and slower defined movements as the players execute the designated pattern of movement directed by the game plan.

Each sport will have its own unique pattern of activity for which your training regimen must be customized.

There are countless ways to train one's body for the power and speed of football. Running hills is a great way to train for speed and power. Hill running is much more demanding than running a flat distance. Rather than run ten forty-yard sprints, some coaches have their football players run ten forty-yard sprints uphill. It is intense and grueling and will test your will and desire to pay the price necessary to accomplish your goal.

There are many times you wonder if it is worth it. For some players, it's the hills that develop the heart. In other players, it's the heart that inspires one to run hills. It's the heart and hills that combine to build a confidence and mental toughness necessary to win a championship.

Whether it's the hills that inspire the heart or the heart that inspires the hills, it is paying the price in the preparation process that determines who receives the prize.

GAME DAY MINDSET

MOST COMPETITORS CAN GIVE
THEIR BEST IN BATTLE ONCE;
IT TAKES A REAL WARRIOR TO
DO IT AGAIN AND AGAIN.

COACH SLOW

Football is a lot like life and life is a lot like football. Obstacles present themselves, challenges must be navigated. Everyone has a game day to face.

The following essays are samples of various mindset messages I created. I would deliver these messages to athletes at the pinnacle of their profession, throughout my NFL coaching career.

They were normally presented the night before competition and I certainly tried to capture the circumstance surrounding the particular battle. Therefore, these do not follow a timeline as each battle presented new circumstances and required different mindsets to gain a competitive edge.

In these pages, I hope you find the inspiration *you* need to give your best as you compete against life's daily battles. May you discover your warrior mindset within, to take on and tackle all the obstacles you encounter.

Success Is Not What You Do for A Living

In my coaching career, I've listened to many athletes proclaim they would do things differently if they were going to be competing for the championship or team championship.

How well they would prepare, practice, play faster, stronger, more consistent, etc.

Each and every time you step on the field, stage, or into a big meeting, you are demonstrating to everyone that you have it in you to be a champion.

Ask yourself this: Will you take what you do for living and every time you compete, live what you do to the fullest?

When you answered "yes" to that question — you are a winner regardless if you ever become a champion.

Successful people live what they do daily.

Others wait for the big game or big stage, or so they say to show how really talented they are.

Success is not WHAT you do for a living, Success is HOW you live what you do!

What Is Success?

I have been a football coach for over thirty-five years and would hear players while watching a playoff or championship game make an interesting comment. "When I get in the playoffs or Super Bowl I will…" My immediate thought was, why wait?

Ask yourself: Will you take what you do for a living and on Game Day live what you do with no regrets? Whatever your Game Day is. Play with heart for sixty minutes. If you can do that you have the heart of a champion and someday you may be called one.

I've known and coached many players who do not have the championship ring or trophy, but are truly champions. We have all heard the phrase *play with heart*. Sometimes what that actually means is taken for granted.

Webster's defines heart two ways: Heart is the emotional aspect of one's innermost character and courage. Another definition: Heart is the strength of mind and will in the face of difficulty.

Regardless what your Game Day is, we can all be champions if we compete in the game of life with Heart!

THE REAL GAME

My favorite time as a coach is in the sanctuary with the players; away from the rest of the world as we prepare for battle.

Rarely does the game of football have lethal consequences. But it does have serious implications for all of those who play the game.

Friends, fans, and media only know the scoreboard, they don't know the real game. The real game holds us accountable in a way that goes beyond our job security, money, and notoriety. Its implications are long-term and they echo into eternity.

The real game doesn't see the scoreboard. The real game sees our soul. In my soul as your coach, the real game finds compassion, love, empathy, and a heart screaming out for success for the guys in the room!

In the real game, when you step across the line onto the field, your actions reflect your heart. In this brotherhood of shared stress, excitement, blood, sweat, and tears we find camaraderie and love. "There is no greater love than to lay down one's life for a friend." (John 15:13)

Not love in the emotional sense and not literally lay down our life. Love in the sense of doing what is right because we are part of a team that depends on us. Laying down our life in the sense of giving our best, day in and day out so as not to let our brothers down. Laying down our life as in each and every snap on game day giving all we have for a friend (the team).

When the final whistle blows, may our actions reflect our heart. When we watch the video, all shall know the truth and the truth shall set us free. Then we will stand in judgement, win or lose, with no regrets!

PLAY WITH PURPOSE

Compete with a meaningful purpose in mind.

Not only for a tangible goal, but something bigger. It's your
heart and soul's desire. It's the substance of all dreams.

Life is filled with competition, adversity, detours, twists, and
turns -- a roller coaster of emotions.

To get the most from life and football you must have strength
and purpose.

Our souls are hungry for something larger than ourselves. We
are hungry to be part of something that has meaning. Hungry
to contribute to making a difference in a positive fashion.[7]

We don't have to have an impact globally, we need only to
make a difference in our own small world. The world only
you and your brotherhood of teammates understand across
those lines into a world of competition most people only
dream of.

We pour our hearts out with our effort not only to find joy in
spite of difficulties, but in the midst of them.[8]

How can you make a difference?

Play each and every snap of your battle with your best effort.

Give your best to a good and common goal so that in victory
or defeat you may stand in judgment with no regrets.

A football game is only sixty minutes but it lasts a lifetime.

As you leave the battlefield, be free from becoming a prisoner
of the thought of a lifetime: "I could've given more!"

ATTITUDE DETERMINES OUTCOME

It all begins in preparation leading up to your battle or
competition.

You've done everything mentally and physically to hone your
skills and absorb the plan for battle.
Now comes what is at times, the most difficult part of
competition.

Now is the time to prepare your heart and soul for what lies
ahead.

It begins well before the game with a thought. I have heard so
often that the team that wants it the most will be the victor.

There are many times I really want something, but I am not
willing to buy it because it will cost more than I want to pay.

Competition is similar.

It begins with a thought, which then becomes a calculation of
what you are willing to pay, and why you will pay.

That calculation brews in the secret place of your mind.
There it brews as it morphs into a resolve that resembles a
quiet thunder.

It stirs your mind in that secret place called the Will.

It finally explodes with passion, focus, and effort:

An effort that is selfless

An effort that cares

An effort of childlike passion

An effort that demands a state of mind that penetrates the soul

An effort based on love
"For there is no greater love than to lay down one's life for a friend." (John 15:13)
Love Always Conquers!

A Special Place

The trip we are going on is to a special place. You can't get there by car, plane, or train.

There is only one way to make this trip and your heart must take you there.

I see you travel there every day. I see you in our meetings. I watch you practice and see you there. This place is REAL. You can get there in an instant. But to do so you must leave everything except your brothers sitting here in this room.

Family and friends you carry with you in your heart always, but they cannot understand where you must go. That's because you are going to a special place between the lines into a world most people only dream of.

Between those lines is a world that demands an intensity of focus and concentration. A world where you must see the smallest details despite the violence and chaos exploding around you.[9]

You must go into a world where words turn into action and your spirit prevails. You can get there in an instant. IT'S A SPECIAL PLACE CALLED ATTITUDE.

A state of mind where regardless of circumstance you do, as Bill Walsh said, "Keep moving, running, hitting, demonstrating your pride, dignity, and defiance."
A defiance to losing and a love for the team!

WHAT WILL BE

The Opponent has seen what we have been. They know not
what we will become.

Regardless of past performance, experience, and emotions,
what WILL be WILL be.

What will be is not determined by the past. Yesterday is gone.

What will be is not controlled by the future. Tomorrow is a
mystery.

What will be is determined by today. Today is the gift we call
the present.

What will be begins in this moment.

What will be comes from our thoughts. It comes from your
hearts and minds in that secret place called the WILL.

Tomorrow's outcome will largely be decided tonight in your
hearts and minds.

*The battle first takes place away from the crowds. Out on
the road and in the gym, in that secret place of the mind
called the will. That is where I have already won long before
I dance under those lights.*
-- Muhammad Ali

What will be is demonstrated on the field by your actions. Reflected by your discipline, passion, and commitment.

What will be is far more powerful than memory of what has been. Now is the time to take the best of what will be and turn it into what IS on the field of competition.

ALL HERE TOGETHER

Some by choice, some by engineered circumstances, somehow, we are all together.

To get to where we want to go we must travel light. "Any man who puts his hand to the plow and looks back is not fit for service." (Luke 9:62)

Keep getting better and keep believing. We all have the same dream. You've honed your skills.

This is your life for a short time. Make the best of this opportunity by giving your best effort. Mother Theresa said, "Life is life, fight for it."

More than talent or intellect, have a passion for good and do good with a passion and you will win!

ANDREA AND MY SON-IN-LAW, ERIC

FOOTBALL IS A TEAM GAME

Football is a game that is no fun when you try playing it in your own world. It's a tough, violent, unforgiving world on the field.

All of you may not be friends. You've come from different parts of the country, different schools, different backgrounds, different interests.

Some of you may not even like one another.

But every one of you belongs to a team. And every one of you belongs, more specifically, to a unit. A defensive unit for example. A linebacker unit, another example.

Just like a family that has fights and some squabbles and difficulties, families survive when things get tough by pulling together.

LEFT TO RIGHT: CAROL'S MOM, ANNE; MY MOM, AUDREY; ANDREA, CAROL AND NATALIE

When you are on the field in this game you are a part of your team. Once you are on the field there's nowhere to hide. There's only you and your teammates. You're on the field for the same reason: to play, to perform, to produce, to win.

Put all your differences aside when you step on the field.

No matter how difficult, impossible, or uncomfortable the circumstance, keep moving, running, and competing. This game is to be played with Heart not Muscle, and Hustle not Speed!

Football Is a Calling

There's a business side of the game where you are paid to play, perform, and produce. That is business, not football.

Football is a calling. To quote a scripture passage, "I heard a voice saying, whom shall I send? Who will go for us?" (Isaiah 6:8)

How does that relate? That call is for everyone, not just a select few. The opponent is being called just as we are. Some do not hear the call. Others will not heed it. Still others respond, then turn back.[10]

Scripture also says many are called but few are chosen because narrow is the gate and difficult is the way that leads to life. You have another opportunity to demonstrate you have chosen to continue. There is something within each of us that determines whether we are going to hear the call. Whether I hear the call and how I respond is based on one thing: Love.

Love is the force that ignites the spirit and binds teams together. When the voice asks, "Whom shall I send? Who will go for us?" Here I am! Send ME! "For there is no greater love than to lay down one's life for a friend."

Love is the catalyst of this small brotherhood where the ties that bind are confidence, mutual respect, shared hazard,

shared fear, and shared triumph. A willingness to obey and a
determination to lead.

The call is for everyone not just a select few. "Whom Shall I
send? Who will go for us?" Here I am, send me.

You are one but not alone; where we go, we go together.

Play the Game

When you have worked your way to reach the highest level of competition, the separation between the top and the bottom is not very far. The mountain top and the valley are only a short distance apart.

From the most sophisticated scheme or tactic to the most tedious, boring aspect of training, the special ingredients are the details.

A great coach not only demands that the details be executed properly, but finds a way to motivate his team or position to make the details their own. When the team invests in themselves and the details that make his work special, the coach and player can reach heights they've never reached before.

A New Journey - Jiu-Jitsu,
ANOTHER PURSUIT SINCE THE COACHING DOOR CLOSED

What kind of work will you sign your name to? The simplest to the most sophisticated aspect of the game can be a Michelangelo piece of art.

To play the game to win there is only one way. Immerse your-self fully in the action.

As Bob Oates Jr. wrote: "Football is a world that demands intensity, involvement, and heightened awareness of the small-est details in an avalanche of experience. Success in this sport, even self-respect demands an intense commitment."[11] And as is written in the Book of Revelation, "It is better to be fiery hot or icy cold, but if you are lukewarm I will spit you out." (Revelation 3:15)

Play each play in and of itself regardless of the circumstances.

There are times when you will be ahead in games and have the urge to let up. If by some chance you are behind, you may have the urge to hang it up.

Fight that urge and play the game and don't let the game play you!

YOUR MOST DANGEROUS MISSION

The most dangerous missions are those when you cannot identify your enemy. We have however, found the real opponent and it is ourselves.

When you cross the lines into your field of battle, carry only the weapons necessary for battle. Anything else is excess baggage and will weigh you down, distracting you from your target.
Your most effective weapons are your effort and brotherhood formed from a common goal.
Recent success or failure can cloud your focus and soften your armor.
The burden of carrying anything mentally or physically that is not necessary for battle will weaken your desire. You must enter again the field of battle.

Most competitors can give their best in battle once, but it takes a real warrior to do it again and again.

Each victory will make the next battle more difficult, more important, and more fierce. Once you've done the physical work, you must go to your secret place of the mind called the will where you decide if you will return to the field as a warrior to answer the call.

Will your effort to battle for as long as the battle ensues and you will slowly win the game. A game where our actions reflect our heart and team spirit prevails!!

ANOTHER ADVENTURE - SUMMER HIKE IN ARIZONA

Escaping the Shadow of Defeat

When adversity strikes over and over, it is easy to close the door and drown in self-pity.

In those difficult times, remember life does not impose itself on you. You select which of life's many offerings you choose to accept.[12]

You can choose between pitiful or powerful. Success is not instant. Success is not even a destination. Success is a choice. A choice that is made over and over again in the secret place of mind called "the will".

When the shadow of defeat lingers, we have all heard the saying *playing for pride*. That the goal or destination is no longer in sight. I beg to differ.

Your goal and what you're playing for is the same goal you started with. Win and loss records are not relevant to motivation or inspiration if you possess the heart of a champion.

A well-known clergyman said that someday in the next year or years you will be wrestling with a great challenge. A bigger battle. But the real struggle is here. Now, in these quiet times.

Now it is being decided whether on the day of your supreme challenge, battle, sorrow, temptation, or game you shall miserably fail or gloriously conquer.

Champions are made through a long, steady, continued process. Leaders cast a vision, but it is the soldier who guarantees the outcome. There are many champions who do not possess the hardware.

WE RISE

Every one of us, as we travel the winding road called life, will find ourselves in circumstances that are bleak.

The vision of where we want to go is possibly beyond our reach. Somewhere within, you search for a reason and purpose to continue to fight.[13]

"Even though the righteous man falls seven times he will rise again." (Proverbs 24:16)

Concern yourself not with past failures, but with the future. Be persistent, determined, and continue to compete and you will transform obstacles into accomplishment.

Your team is forged and molded by the brotherhood of mutual respect, shared hazard, shared fear, confidence, shared triumph, accountability, and love.

It is love that ignites the spirit and binds teams together.

There is real meaning in your game, whatever your game is beyond the outcome. A meaning only one who is part of a team-related venture can fully understand.

"There is no greater love than to lay down one's life for a friend." (John 15:13)

Not literally, but doing what is right for the team day in and day out.

In all circumstances, continue to battle, demonstrating your commitment to a purpose larger than any tangible reward could ever be!

Always a Contender

There are those who say it can't be done and are content to leave it at that.

And there are those who find a way.

There are those who see every setback as an excuse to give up.

And there are those who find the courage, the will, the commitment to persevere.

There are those who skim along life's path, and there are those who dive in deeply.

That is where meaning, purpose, vision, and truth are clear and unmistakable.

There are those who have been blessed with every advantage and wind up with nothing to show for it.

Others have been saddled with an unimaginable burden, yet have risen to magnificent heights.

As the game plays out, whatever the moments may bring, make the choice to look at the positive possibilities. This day, this moment, this life is what you make of it.

Run toward your challenges and you'll be running toward true achievement. Challenges are not there to stop you. They are there to make you stronger. You are always a contender regardless of circumstance.

The goal is the championship -- whether it is this year, next year, or the next.

When you take what you do for a living and live what you do and play with heart, you build the heart of a champion and someday may become one!

Dear Teammate

I write this letter in hopes you as my teammates have an opportunity to read it before we cross the lines onto the playing field to do battle.

All of us must deal with our fears, anxieties, apprehensions, and stress.

In my case and most likely in yours, I'm not speaking of serious injury or losing the game.

My biggest fear is failing to do that for which I have so passionately trained. In the heat of battle or competition, letting my teammates down.

I have made my spiritual peace and in the secret place of my mind called the Will, counted the cost I am willing to pay.

We have already paid the price in preparation. In order to obtain the prize we do not have, we must go to where we have nothing. Travel light and carry only the thoughts necessary for the competition or battle.

Compete one moment at a time. The last moment is gone, future moments uncertain.

Live and focus in the present moment. Play as though there is no game clock. Effort is your weapon.

Give your best effort every moment until there is none to give. It is at that point you will realize that buried beneath our fears and anxieties is love for one another.

Not love in the emotional sense, but love meaning giving our best, moment after moment, doing what is right day after day, laying it on the line play after play.

Realizing we are not playing to win only the scoreboard, but fighting for something bigger than ourselves. It is here you realize the times you are most alive and truly enjoy walking between the lines with these teammates and offering yourself to the team out of the spirit of love.

We fight not for the scoreboard but for one another and that gives us a sense of peace, pride, and FIGHT!

THE CHAMPIONSHIP GAME

This is the day. It's time.

You set your sights on the goal.

It's now time to go beyond planning and thinking.

This is the day. This is the time to prove we are the choice ones.

But it is here in clear sight of the vision, most turn back.

Many become clouded by complacency, distractions, and the grind of the process. The comfort of past successes dulls the edge and softens the armor.

Every bit of your training has been in the direction of the vision. What is behind you and what is ahead of you is not nearly as important as what is within you.

Life is never easy. It is always the hard road.

Real opportunities to become the best are few. These precious opportunities are not to be feared. Do not worry about what might be lost. You cannot lose what you do not yet have.

Consider what it is you have that you may give. This is the day you celebrate your good fortune by using the talent you have been blessed with for the common good of your team.

To give of yourself to something bigger than you could ever do alone.

Commit your mind and spirit to battle in that secret place called the Will. It is there where you must count the cost. Count the cost and be at peace to give all you have on the field.

This is the day to give of yourself to the team. More than talent or intellect, passion and spirit will prevail.

NO BOUNDARIES

As I JOURNEY on from my NFL and collegiate coaching careers, I have thrown myself into some new activities and immersed myself in stimulating my intellectual curiosity. While navigating the path I also came upon a profound self-revelation.

You can take the coach from football, but you can't take football from the coach! I am as excited and passionate about my new ventures as I have ever been. I realize that you don't have to coach in the NFL, college, or high school to be a coach. I have the freedom of time and the curiosity to delve into the oldest and newest of X and O strategies and tactics.

FROM NFL STATE-OF-THE-ART FACILITIES, TO A GARAGE OFFICE

Coaching to me has always been more than Xs and Os and wins and losses.

IT'S NOT WHERE YOU WORK,
IT'S THE PASSION YOU WORK WITH!

Coaching means seeking a way to help others compete at their highest possible level; no matter their field of battle.

I hope to continue doing that by sharing the experiences and many lessons I have learned during my coaching career.

In this world full of good and bad, I choose to continuously search for the good. As I dive deeply into the ocean of experience earned from my career, I will also share from an abundance of new experiences. My current coaching career is one with no boundaries but my own.

ME AND MY WIFE, CAROL

About the Coach

A TWENTY-YEAR CAREER in the NFL, a member of a Super Bowl Championship team, and nine years as a defensive coordinator provided a unique perspective on leadership.

A defensive coordinator reports to a head coach. The position therefore offers the vantage point of both a leader and a team member. This awareness lends the ability to impart lessons on how to lead with the understanding of what it's like to be led – all under the bright lights of the big leagues.

Over the course of his thirty-five-year football career, Bob spent time in the company of people at their best and at their worst. He saw how they responded to success and how they extended their humanity; on- and off-camera. His was that rarefied experience of life in the NFL.

Bob and his wife Carol are the proud parents of four children: Ryan, Andrea, Bobby, and Steven.

Acknowledgements

I N SOME WAYS, we become a product of our experiences. As I competed in my journey through coaching, an abundant desire to touch more people than the small groups I coached grew stronger. I developed a passion to pass on messages that might inspire anyone looking for hope in the toughest game of all – life. This desire lay dormant as I pursued my coaching passion. When the door closed on that career, my wish to coach in a different way took form.

The encouragement of my wife, Carol and my brother, Brian instilled the confidence I needed to take on my new venture.

A special thanks to Mary Dado whose expertise and friendship pushed me through all obstacles. Without Mary, this book would never have made it to print. A thank you also to Rosie my niece, for all her hard work.

I've crossed paths with so many special coaches and players on my coaching journey. I couldn't possibly list them all. These are only a few of many who have influenced who and what I have become.

My friend Steve Mooney: My inspiration as a late bloomer
Mike Shanahan: Offensive Play Calling Genius
Jimmy Johnson: Brilliant
Dave Wannstedt: Natural Born Leader, Great Football Mind
Ron Wolf: King of Talent Acquisition
Mike Sherman: Organizational Master, Tireless
Champ Bailey: Best Player I've Ever Coached
London Fletcher: Warrior
John Lynch: Ultimate Competitor

To all the other coaches I've worked for or with and all the players I've coached, it was truly an honor and I thank you!

Whether you're actively coaching or have coaching aspirations, wish to highlight a cause you champion, or want to join this community to motivate and inspire others to do good — it takes a team. Together we thrive.

Join us, follow us, share your stories with us on social media.

On Facebook
Facebook.com/bobslowik92/

On Twitter
@coach_slow

On YouTube
CoachSlow.com

On LinkedIn
linkedin.com/in/bobslowik/

If you are interested in learning about custom coaching clinics or just need help keeping your head in the game, let us know!

-- Coach Slow
www.CoachSlow.com

REFERENCES AND NOTES

While a natural inclination, my passion to inspire those I've coached and those I've yet to meet is fueled by reading the motivational works of hundreds of thought and spiritual leaders like John C. Maxwell and Oswald Chambers.

I reference them throughout this book, both directly and indirectly; quoted to the absolute best of my ability. I am fortunate to have internalized their wisdom. I am a stronger, more evolved person because of their teachings.

Although I never met any of you, you have been there when I needed you. Thank you.

1   Oswald Chambers, *My Utmost for His Highest* (Discovery House Publishers, 2005)

2   Bob Oates Jr., *A Game of Passion* (Distributed by Scribner; First Edition, 1975)

3   Carlos Castaneda, *The Teachings of Don Juan: A Yaqui Way of Knowledge* (Published 1983 by Touchstone/Simon & Schuster - First published 1968)

4   Gary Barnett, *High Hopes* (Grand Central Publishing, 2009)

5   John Whitmore, *Coaching for Performance: GROWing Human Potential and Purpose: The Principles and Practice of Coaching and Leadership* (Nicholas Brealey Publishing, 2010)

6   Mary Stevenson, *Footprints in the Sand* (Poem written in 1936)

7   John C. Maxwell and Jim Dornan, *Becoming a Person of Influence* (Publisher: Thomas Nelson, 2006)

8   Oswald Chambers, *My Utmost for His Highest* (Discovery House Publishers, 2005)

9   Bob Oates Jr., *A Game of Passion* (Distributed by Scribner; First Edition, 1975)

10 Oswald Chambers, *My Utmost for His Highest* (Discovery House Publishers, 2005)

11 Bob Oates Jr., *A Game of Passion* (Distributed by Scribner; First Edition, 1975)

12 Joyce Meyer, *Ending Your Day Right* (Publisher: Warner Faith; 1st Warner Books Ed Edition, 2004)

13 Oswald Chambers, *My Utmost for His Highest* (Discovery House Publishers, 2005)